Souls in Harmony

THE DEVOTIONAL WORKBOOK FOR A JOY-FILLED MARRIAGE

LOVE ABIDING BOOKS

Copyright © 2020 by Love Abiding Books

All rights reserved. No part of this book may be reproduced or used in any manner without written permission of the copyright owner except for the use of quotations in a book review. For more information, address: info@ loveabiding.club

FIRST EDITION

www.loveabiding.club

Your Free Gift

To thank you for you purchase, get your free
Love Abiding Journal

If you want to benefit from this book long term, and I'm pretty sure that is the goal, I cannot emphasize strongly enough that writing down your thoughts and reflections on every chapter is essential. Keeping track of the tasks both for now and for later will be a great encouragment and help. That's why we created a **devotional journal**. It's easy to follow with all the weekly tasks in this book with enough extra space. Extra convenient if you want to keep seperate notes, or if you prefer to not make notes in the book.

Give your relationship the attention it deserves!

INSTANT FREE DOWNLOAD AT :
www.loveabiding.club/journal

Table of Contents

Your Free Gift .... *iii*
Week One : My Favorite Story is Ours *5*
Week Two: Because of You, God *11*
Week Three: The Little Engine That Stays Married *16*
Week Four: That's What Forgiveness Looks Like *21*
Week Five: Beauty and the Beast *26*
Week Six: It's a Date *31*
Week Seven: Through The Years *37*
Week Eight: I Choose Happy *43*
Week Nine: Because God Wants Me To *48*
Week Ten: A Healthy Dose of Fear *56*
Week Eleven: You'll Shoot Your Eye Out *62*
Week Twelve: Hold My Hand…Not a Grudge *68*
Week Thirteen:
Praise God from Whom All Blessings of Marriage Flow *73*
Week Fourteen:
The Couple That Prays and Plays Together Stays Together *79*
Week Fifteen: It's the Thought That Counts *84*
Week Sixteen: Marriage Is… *90*
Week Seventeen: When Mr. Satan Knocks *95*
Week Eighteen: The Etiquette of Thankfulness *100*
Week Nineteen: It's All About That 'Tude *105*
Week Twenty: Priorities…Priorities…Priorities *111*
Week Twenty-one: Accountability Factor *117*
Week Twenty-two: I Did and I Still Do *122*
Week Twenty-three: Listen to Your Body *128*
Week Twenty-four: Fingernails on the Chalkboard *136*
Week Twenty-five: Because *142*
Week Twenty-six: In Times Like These *149*
Week Twenty-seven: Road Work Ahead *158*
Week Twenty-eight: It's Okay to Ask for Help *166*
Week Twenty-nine: When One + One + One Doesn't Equal One .. *173*
Week Thirty: Romance Rekindled *177*
Week Thirty-one: A Slow Leak *182*
Week Thirty-two: Praying Your Way to Happiness *187*
Week Thirty-three: The Family Meeting *195*
Week Thirty-four: M & M's (Majors and Minors) *201*
Week Thirty-five: Change it Up *208*

Week Thirty-six: Eewwww, Yuk! *217*
Week Thirty-seven: Trading Places..................................*223*
Week Thirty-eight: Let's Talk…No, Let's Really Talk *229*
Week Thirty-nine: The Best Things in Life Aren't Things *238*
Week Forty: I'm…sorry *244*
Week Forty-one: You Are My Everything *250*
Week Forty-two: More Than Just Roommates............................*258*
Week Forty-three: Me Days *266*
Week Forty-four: Thanks for Making Me…..............................*275*
Week Forty-five: Don't Jump *282*
Week Forty-six: Better Together *289*
Week Forty-seven: Relaaaaax *295*
Week Forty-eight: The Buck Stops Here *304*
Week Forty-nine: Spring Cleaning *312*
Week Fifty: It's not All About Either of You.............................*318*
Week Fifty-one: Close to You *325*
Week Fifty-two: In Pursuit of Love *332*
Closing Comments: Fifty-two weeks...*337*

Foreword

I don't know for sure how many books there are on the subject of marriage, but I'm sure the term 'a lot' would be an accurate one. And among all those books are devotionals for couples—books that encourage and challenge husbands and wives to put (and keep) God at the center of their own lives and the life of their marriage. So why write another one? Great question, and one I'm more than happy to answer.

Reason number one: No matter how many books there are out there, that number is nowhere near 50% (of all books). On the other hand, 50% of all marriages (give or take a fraction of a percentage) fail. I'd say that's a pretty clear indication we still need help.

Reason number two: I care about marriage. I care about your marriage. I know I don't even know you, but we are brothers and sisters in Christ, which makes us family. And I care about family. So, by writing this book, I am reaching out as a brother in Christ and mentor of sorts.

Reason number three: Marriage, like the rest of the universe, was created by God, which means the only way it can work as wonderfully and wholly as it is meant to, is to do it God's way. We live in a society that thinks nothing about ignoring God's intention and design for marriage. In fact, it's not an exaggeration to say marriage God's way is under attack. As Christians, we have a responsibility to speak up to and stand firm against anyone or anything that threatens to make marriage anything other than what God created it to be in the first place.

That's the 'why' of this book. Now for the 'what'…
The word 'devotional', obviously comes from the word 'devotion'. A few of the synonyms (words that are similar in meaning) for the word 'devotion' are attentiveness, loyalty, fidelity, attachment, adoration, commitment, constancy, and love.
Each and every single one of the words listed there could be used to describe the message we receive from God's Word, the Bible, concerning God's involvement in our lives, AND what he expects us to give back to him. But guess what else those words should be able to describe? Our marriages—both what we give and what we receive from our spouse. That's why it makes perfect sense to combine the two.
Souls is a combination of sound Biblical teaching combined with situations, testimonies, and solutions from married couples living the same kind of lives you are. There are 52 devotions—one for each week of the year, so as not to cause you to feel hurried or stressed to keep up on a daily basis.
Each week's devotion touches on a specific theme or topic; using a verse or verses from the Bible to steer you toward a God-centered approach and way of thinking. Along with scripture, you will hear from people just like you who have been-there-done-that, and who want to offer encouragement and advice for remaining devoted to God and to each other. Each week's devotion will conclude with a bit of a homework assignment—practical and doable actions and applications for the purpose of taking your marriage to its fullest potential. But be warned: all the actions and applications in the world won't help if YOU don't them. Or at least try.
Last but not least, let's look at the 'how' of Souls in Harmony. It's a devotional workbook for couples with a strong emphasis

on doing small tasks every week. It is most effective if both the husband and wife are on board, after all, marriage is a partnership. By reading, talking, praying, and working together, a closer connection and tighter bond is unavoidable. You won't be able to stop it, because (as scripture says) what God joins together, man won't be able to separate.

If, however, your spouse can't or won't read the book or do the homework with you, please do not let that stop you. Some of you may be married to unbelievers. Some of you may have a spouse who loves the LORD, but whose spiritual maturity isn't at a place where they see the benefits of doing something like this together. Some of you may have a spouse who is deployed overseas, or whose job takes them away frequently. If so, that's all the more reason to take God-focused steps to protect and enhance your marriage.

Don't be afraid to step out in faith to make your marriage stronger and more vital. Remember what it says in 1st Peter 3:1—that a Christian wife's actions and attitude (or Christian husband's) can win the heart of her husband (or his wife) to the LORD.

You also need to know that…

There is no wrong time to begin. It doesn't follow the calendar year, so if you want to start Week 1 in September after the kids go back to school, go for it!

Each devotion is only one or one and one-half pages long. It will take less time to read and reflect on this than you spend reading your email or Facebook feed. And it goes without saying it will be time better spent.

The 'homework' will never ask you to strain even the tightest of budgets, try to find more time in the day, or do anything you shouldn't already be doing (or saying) in your marriage. What the homework will do, however, is cause you to remember, respond vs. react, and revel in the fact that your marriage is a 'place' where words like love, nurture, cherished, faithful, and respect ring true.

Oh, and did I say love? That's okay—it's worth repeating.

Week One : My Favorite Story is Ours

Isaac brought her into the tent of his mother Sarah, and he married Rebekah. So she became his wife, and he loved her… ~Genesis 24:67a

John was fourteen and Darla was fifteen when John's family moved to town. Darla's grandma saw the new family sitting in church and said, "Darla you need to be nice to that boy. He looks like a nice boy—just sad because he had to leave his friends, his school, and everything else. It can't be easy being the new kid in town. Besides," she added, "he might just end up asking you out on a date when you're older." Darla wasn't impressed, but she was obedient—to God and her grandma—so she invited John to youth group. He said no…the first time. And the second. But the third attempt proved successful and pretty soon the two became good friends. Friendship turned into love, and love turned into marriage, four kids, seven grandkids, and 44 years (so far) filled with happiness, sadness, fear, excitement, pain, laughter, sickness and death, worries, anger, resolution, joy, hard work, fun, and lots and lots and lots of love, faith, and Jesus. "We're living our version of 'happily ever after'," Darla says. What? Pain, death, and fear sure don't sound very happily ever after-ish. Or do they? Think about it—our faith and our relationship with God won't grow and thrive unless we get the full experience. In other words, faith isn't really faith until it's all that holds us together, and we don't really understand the depth of God's love until we let him love us His way. The same is true in your marriage. Your story, aka your 'happily ever after' is only truly happy when you know your love is sustainable. When your faith in God and each other are all that's holding you together, and when the vows you took aren't just words, but your daily to-do list, you'll know your story is being co-authored by you, your spouse, and God. And what a story it will be! Isaac and Rebekah's story started out as a story of love and admiration but turned to one of horrific deception and dysfunction. Yet we read in Genesis 26:35, these two were once again of one heart and mind, which tells us that they didn't give up on God or each other. The last line of their story was, "…until death did us part." What about you? What do you want the next chapters of your story to say? Do it for yourself and for each other.

Prayer

LORD, thank you for my husband/wife. Thank you for bringing us together and for the joy and fulfillment our marriage brings to our lives. Keep your hand on the pen that writes our story, so that it will be a story of love—for you and for one another.

TASK 1

Spend some time together this week recalling how you met, what first attracted you to each other, and when you first realized you wanted to spend the rest of your life together.

_____
_____
_____
_____
_____
_____
_____
_____
_____
_____
_____
_____
_____
_____
_____
_____
_____
_____
_____

Week One : My Favorite Story is Ours

TASK 2

WRITE DOWN WHAT YOU FEEL ARE THE HIGHS AND LOWS OF YOUR STORY (YOUR MARRIAGE). COMPARE LISTS AND TALK ABOUT WHY YOU WROTE THE THINGS YOU DID, THE SPEND TIME PRAYING TOGETHER; THANKING GOD FOR THE HIGHS AND FOR HIS PROTECTION AND STRENGTH THAT GOT YOU THROUGH THE LOWS.

TASK 3

How do you want future chapters of your story to read? Spend time this week sharing your hopes and dreams, your concerns, and goals you would like to achieve—both individually and as a couple.

_____

_____

_____

_____

_____

_____

_____

_____

_____

_____

_____

_____

_____

_____

_____

_____

Week One : My Favorite Story is Ours

Week Two: Because of You, God

Husbands, love your wives, just as Christ loved the church and gave himself up for her. ~Ephesians 5:25

When thinking about the level of sacrificial love Christ has for the Church—that he willingly died so that the Church could live—I can't help but think that the marriages of military couples are somewhat similar.

A solider give us, aka sacrifices his (or her) comfort, time with family, missing out on lots of firsts, and so many other things out of love for this country and for his (or her) family's welfare, and ours, too. The sacrifices don't end there, though. The soldier's wife (or husband) and children also make quite a few sacrifices. Military spouses often find themselves filling the role of both parents, going for day and weeks without seeing or hearing from the love of their life, juggling delayed pay, getting settled in a house and school just in time to pack up and do it all again, and a lot more. But they do it with a smile on their face and joy in their hearts because they love their husband (or wife), they love this country, and they are proud of their family's role in keeping us all safe and free.

It's easy to see the parallels, isn't it? But as selfless and sacrificial as our military families are, the sacrificial selflessness of Jesus

Christ is immeasurably greater. The sacrifices of Christ are greater because they are eternal and unconditional. Jesus' sacrifice is also a deeply personal act between him and every individual. We can never repay Jesus for what all he has done (and still does), but the beauty of it all is that he doesn't expect us to. All he asks is that we live grateful lives. And the best way to show our gratitude is to walk in his footsteps. Live the way he lived and loved the way he loves.

This week's verse is a crystal-clear picture of what loving like Jesus loves is meant to look like in our marriage.

- Imitators of Christ
- Devoted
- Selfless
- Willing
- Sacrificial
- Going the distance, with no distance being too far

Take a couple of minutes to really look at each of those words and think about what they mean in a marriage. What they bring to the table in a marriage. I don't think there's a man or woman out there that would push a mate away for being that kind of spouse. Do you? So think about it—if you long for a spouse like that, don't you think your husband or wife is, too?

Prayer

LORD, thank you for giving us such a clear picture of what your desire for marriage is. Help us to be an example of what you intend marriage to be. In the name of Jesus, amen.

Week Two: Because of You, God

TASK 1

Write down each of the words you just looked at on a piece of paper. Imitators of Christ, devoted, selfless, willing, sacrifical, going the distance. Next to each one, write down two or three things you can do to demonstrate this characteristic of love to your spouse. Now, trade lists and circle the one thing next to each word you most desire your spouse to do for you.

TASK 2 TIME THIS WEEK TO PRAY NOT ONLY FOR YOUR MARRIAGE, BUT FOR THE MARRIAGES OF OUR MILITARY FAMILIES. ASK GOD TO PROTECT THEM FROM PHYSICAL HARM, AS WELL AS THE EMOTIONAL AND MENTAL STRESSES THAT ARE PART OF THEIR LIVES..

Week Two: Because of You, God

TASK 3

STARTING THIS WEEK, GET IN THE HABIT OF ASKING YOUR SPOUSE AT LEAST ONCE A WEEK, "WHAT CAN I DO TO MAKE YOUR DAY EASIER?"

_____
_____
_____
_____
_____
_____
_____
_____
_____
_____
_____
_____
_____
_____
_____
_____
_____
_____
_____
_____

Souls in Harmony

Week Three: The Little Engine That Stays Married

And let us not grow weary of doing good, for in due season we will reap, if we do not give up. ~Galatians 6:9

"It's a miracle he's even alive," the doctors told Jake's wife, Nicole. "The burns are pretty severe, and a mere two inches from his heart. We'll need to monitor him for some things that aren't uncommon following an injury like his," the doctor continued, "but like I said, it's a miracle he's still here." The burns they doctor was talking about were electrical burns. Jake, a lineman, had been electrocuted when strong winds snapped a damaged pole and a 'hot' wire whipped across his body. Jake and Nicole were most definitely thankful he was alive, but when he was released from the hospital a couple of weeks later, Nicole realized the scars from the burns were not nearly as bad as the emotional and mental scars. Anxiety, irritability, sullenness, secluding himself from her and their two small boys, constant worrying and complaining…. Jake was no longer the gentle, funny, good-natured man she had married. And it terrified her. Determined not to let the miracle God gave them go to waste, Nicole refused to let the damage done to her husband damage their marriage. She refused to reciprocate with the same pessimism, anger, and sulking he doled out to her and the boys. No way was she going down that easy! "Why are you so nice to me? Why do just keep letting me treat you like this?"

Jake yelled at his wife after she asked him the same thing she'd asked every day since the accident: "What can I do to make your day easier and better?" "Because I love you. I love us. And I'm not going to let anything steal the miracle God gave us," Nicole whispered. "I'm just not." Jake was humbled by his wife's steadfast commitment. He knew in that moment "…for better or worse, in sickness and in health…" were more than just words to the woman he'd married, and that knowledge gave him the motivation he needed to try to get the help he needed to be fully recovered. The recovery process wasn't an easy one. There are still times when PTSD rears its ugly head, but because Nicole didn't grow weary in doing what was good and right for her marriage, she and Jake, as well as their children, are reaping the rewards of faithfulness. She believed God's promise in this week's verse—that there are blessings to be had when we don't give up or give in to the temptation to get even or put up a shield of defense. Jake and Nicole's situation was more extreme than most, but if they can realize the truth of God's promise to reap a marriage filled with goodness, kindness, and tender, loving care, you can to. So go ahead—decide today to ask your spouse this question every single day: "What can I do to make your day better?" And then do it.

Prayer

LORD, give me a heart and eyes that always seeks and always desires to do good in my marriage. Help me realize that by doing good, I am bringing good to those I love and honor to you. Amen.

TASK 1 WHAT ARE SOME OF THE ANSWERS YOU WILL GIVE YOUR SPOUSE WHEN THEY ASK YOU THIS QUESTION?

_____
_____
_____
_____
_____
_____
_____
_____
_____
_____
_____
_____
_____
_____
_____
_____
_____
_____
_____
_____

Week Three: The Little Engine That Stays Married

TASK 2

Take a few minutes to think back to some special moments you shared. Your first date. Where were you when you first said, "I love you"? What was the first gift he gave you? She gave you? Recreate these memories and spend time remembering the past while looking forward to the future.

_____
_____
_____
_____
_____
_____
_____
_____
_____
_____
_____
_____
_____
_____
_____
_____
_____
_____
_____
_____

TASK 3
HOW DO YOU THINK BEING MORE CONSCIOUS OF ENHANCING EACH OTHER'S DAYS WILL AFFECT YOUR RELATIONSHIP? IN OTHER WORDS, WHAT WILL YOU REAP?

_____
_____
_____
_____
_____
_____
_____
_____
_____
_____
_____
_____
_____
_____
_____
_____
_____
_____
_____

Week Three: The Little Engine That Stays Married

Week Four: That's What Forgiveness Looks Like

Therefore, as God's chosen people, holy and dearly loved, clothe yourselves with compassion, kindness, humility, gentleness and patience. Bear with each other and forgive one another if any of you has a grievance against someone. Forgive as the Lord forgave you. And over all these virtues put on love, which binds them all together in perfect unity. ~Colossians 3:12-14

Victoria forgave Bill when he confessed that he'd been having an affair but realized she (Victoria) and their children were far to precious to lose. The couple went forward in church the following Sunday so that Bill could make a public confession and ask for prayer and help in healing. Nearly 40 years later, these two are still happily married and about to become great-grandparents! That's what forgiveness looks like. Kara was able to hide the evidence of her secret spending habits until the mortgage company called her husband saying they were six months in arrears. Marcus thought it had to be a mistake. It wasn't. Long story short, they lost their house, no one wanted to rent to someone with such poor credit, and Marcus almost lost his job over the whole situation. When a friend asked Marcus if he'd filed for divorce yet, Marcus said, "You have no idea how hurt I am, but at the end of the day, she means more to me than any house ever could."

The couple went through intense counseling and twenty-five years later they are still very happily married. That's what forgiveness looks like.

Jared and Mackenzie have a solid Christian marriage. But when Mackenzie's dad died, Jared didn't know how to reach out to her. His lack of understanding caused him to say things like "Death is part of life. You know that, so you need to move on and be thankful you'll see him again someday." and "At least you had a dad who cared."

Mackenzie was deeply hurt by Jared's lack of compassion and caring. When she finally confronted Jared about his callousness and lack of compassion, he admitted his wrongdoing and to feeling jealous that she had a dad to grieve. "My dad has been dead to me since I was seven. At least you got to say goodbye. I barely even got to say hello."

Mackenzie readily forgave Jared because she realized his loss was at least as significant has hers, yet no one had ever told him he could/should grieve his loss. So they grieved the loss of both their dads together. That's what forgiveness looks like.

If you have accepted Jesus' gift of salvation, you have been called to put on Christ…to be like him. And that includes a willingness to forgive your spouse just like Jesus Christ has forgiven you.

Prayer

Father in heaven, forgive my unforgiveness and take it from me. Help me remember that forgiveness is at the heart of love. In the name of Jesus, amen.

TASK 1

ARE YOU HARBORING RESENTMENT AND UNFORGIVENESS TOWARD YOUR SPOUSE ABOUT ANYTHING... BIG OR SMALL? WHY HAVE YOU NOT FORGIVEN THEM FOR THESE THINGS?

_____
_____
_____
_____
_____
_____
_____
_____
_____
_____
_____
_____
_____
_____
_____
_____
_____
_____
_____

TASK 2

What about you? What have you said or done to hurt your spouse? If you have not asked them to forgive you, why haven't you?

_____
_____
_____
_____
_____
_____
_____
_____
_____
_____
_____
_____
_____
_____
_____
_____
_____
_____
_____

TASK 3

Often times it's the not-so-little little things that causes resentment and an unforgiving spirit to take root and spread like poison ivy in our marriage. Take some time praying together for openness, gracious honesty, and forgiving hearts. Then spend some time alone asking God to cleanse your heart from any ill-will and resentment; replacing it with that deep, forever love God wants us to have for our spouse.

Week Five: Beauty and the Beast

But the Lord said to Samuel, "Do not look on his appearance or on the height of his stature, because I have rejected him. For the Lord sees not as man sees: man looks on the outward appearance, but the Lord looks on the heart." ~1st Samuel 16:7 ESV

Are you familiar with Disney's "Beauty and the Beast"? That's probably a silly question, but just in case you aren't, here it is in a nutshell… Gaston, the village's most eligible bachelor, has decided he wants Belle, the prettiest girl in the village, to be his wife. Gaston is of the opinion that Belle will jump at the chance, because, well, because why wouldn't she? He's…he's Gaston, for goodness sakes! There's just one little thing Gaston didn't count on, though. Belle wants nothing to do with him. She has no feelings for him whatsoever, so his good looks, the warm, rustic lodge he calls home, and all the other qualities he thinks make him the perfect 'catch', are complete turnoffs to Belle. And then there's the beast… Handsome is the last word you would use to describe his scruffy, wild, and wooly appearance. He's belligerent, gruff, rude, and just downright mean. Yet for all that, there's something about the guy Belle likes. Even though he infuriates her and yes, scares her (a little), her intuition tells her not to give up.

Over time, that something Belle felt turns to love.

She doesn't see a beast. She sees the one she wants to share her life with. At first the beast doesn't think it's possible that Belle loves him. How could she? He knows what he looks like! How he's behaved for the past however many years! Belle proves to him, however, that none of that matters—that she doesn't see any of that. All she sees is who he is from the inside out. And yes, as is the case with any good Disney movie, Beauty (Belle) and the Beast live happily ever after.

This week's verse is God's way of saying you and your husband or wife need to write your own version of Beauty and the Beast. You need to see each other from the inside out, so that you see who you are married to. By the same token, however, you need to make sure your heart and mind truly are the beautiful organs God created. You need to be beautiful from the inside out, i.e. kind, compassionate, forgiving, patient, gentle, thoughtful, honest, tender, attentive....

Simply put, you need to be your best self and see your spouse's best self. You need to see yourself and your spouse the way God sees you—from the inside out.

CAUTION: I also want to warn you to carefully guard your vision. Don't let yourself look at other marriages, other women, or other men in comparison. Your marriage's theme song needs to be the 1959 hit song by the Flamingos titled, "I Only Have Eyes For You".

Prayer

God, thank you for creating me in your image. Help me, though, to do my best to be a true reflection of you. Help me to be loving and kind, and to see my spouses' faults through a lens of love. In the name of Jesus, amen.

TASK 1

JAMES 3:2 A SAYS, FOR WE ALL STUMBLE IN MANY WAYS. WHEN HAVE YOU BEEN GUILTY OF FOCUSING ON YOUR SPOUSE'S FLAWS, BUT IGNORING YOUR OWN?

_____
_____
_____
_____
_____
_____
_____
_____
_____
_____
_____
_____
_____
_____
_____
_____
_____
_____

Week Five: Beauty and the Beast

TASK 2

Ask each other, "What do you see when you look at me?" None of us is perfect, so don't be afraid to let your spouse know about something that bothers you. Just be sure you do it gently and with sincere kindness.

TASK 3

What three things irritate you about yourself or cause you to feel insecure about yourself? Share the list with your spouse and talk about your answers. Use the time to build each other up.

_____
_____
_____
_____
_____
_____
_____
_____
_____
_____
_____
_____
_____
_____
_____
_____
_____
_____
_____

Week Six: It's a Date

Let your fountain be blessed, and rejoice in the wife of your youth, a lovely deer, a graceful doe. Let her breasts fill you at all times with delight; be intoxicated always in her love. ~Proverbs 5:18-19 ESV

That's pretty mushy talk for the Bible, isn't it? (said tongue in cheek). Of course the Bible can talk about romance and sex! God invented both of them, and since the Bible tells us that everything God created is good, we need to stop seeing romance and sex as something the world invented. Have you ever seen an elderly couple walking through the mall? Were any of them holding hands and talking to each other? Or were they pinch-faced and silent? Or what about in a restaurant? Do you notice couples who are smiling and having a conversation? The guys who hold the door for their lady, or help her with her coat? It's not hard to pick out the couples who enjoy being together, is it? But would you like to know why they enjoy being together? It's because they do it on a regular basis. They enjoy it. They want to be together. They take pleasure in making each other smile. It's oh, so easy to let the busy-ness and business of being married bury the romantic, fun parts of marriage. Work, raising kids, keeping the lawn mowed and the laundry done, juggling schedules, sneaking in a shower before your toddler discovers where you're at, taking on extra hours to try to save up for a down payment on a house or to pay off student loans, caring for aging parents, dealing with a rebellious teenager, babysitting the grandkids while everyone else goes to work…all of these things are either necessary, good, or both. But they're not the only things that matter.

YOU AND YOUR SPOUSE MATTER. ROMANCE MATTERS. INTIMACY AND SEX MATTER.

The Bible devoted an entire book (Song of Songs) to the subject of romance and intimacy between a married couple. It's important to God, so if it's important to him, it needs to be important to us, too. God says we are to be one with each other. He's not just talking about physical oneness. He's talking about emotional oneness, too—the kind that comes from talking about anything but the kids and household stuff. The kind that comes from holding hands, cuddling, laughing over a funny movie, enjoying the sights and sounds of Christmas together, crying together at the loss of a friend or family member, sharing old memories and making new ones. And yes, even being able to finish each other's sentences (at least once in a while).

Making date nights a priority is a must for a healthy marriage. Think about it—you can't truly be happy or be lovingly devoted to someone you don't know or enjoy spending time with. So do yourselves a favor and be the kind of one God wants you to be. One in body, heart, and mind.

Prayer

God, open my heart and mind's eyes to make my marriage a priority—second only to you. Help me realize the importance of valuing and cherishing my mate and the time we spend together. In the name of Jesus, amen.

TASK 1 CHOOSE FROM THE FOLLOWING AND GO ON A DATE THIS WEEK: ICE CREAM OR FROZEN YOGURT WHILE SOMEONE WATCHES THE KIDS; A HIGH SCHOOL FOOTBALL GAME; ROLLER SKATING; BOWLING; WALKING TRAILS AT THE PARK; STAYING HOME AND PLAYING BOARD GAMES (NO SCREENS OR PHONES ALLOWED); RECREATE YOUR FIRST DATE; ACT LIKE A TOURIST IN YOUR OWN TOWN.

TASK 2

PUT A CUTE JAR, BASKET, OR PIGGY BANK SOMEWHERE IN THE HOUSE THAT IS CONVENIENT FOR DUMPING SPARE CHANGE IN. EMPTY IT OUT ONCE A MONTH AND SPEND IT ON A DATE NIGHT.

Week Six: It's a Date

TASK 3

IF YOU HAVE CHILDREN STILL AT HOME, MAKE A LIST OF YOUR FRIENDS WHO ARE IN THE SAME BOAT. SET UP A SCHEDULE FOR TRADING BABYSITTING SO EACH COUPLE CAN ENJOY DATE NIGHTS WITHOUT HAVING TO PAY A SITTER.

TASK 4

SET SPECIFIC DATES EACH MONTH (NO LESS THAN 2) FOR DATE NIGHTS. FOR EXAMPLE, THE FIRST FRIDAY AND THIRD SUNDAY AFTERNOON OF EACH MONTH. MAKE THESE NON-NEGOTIABLE EXCEPT IN THE EVENT OF A FAMILY EMERGENCY OR ILLNESS.

Week Six: It's a Date

Week Seven: Through The Years

He answered, "Have you not read that he who created them from the beginning made them male and female, and said, 'Therefore a man shall leave his father and his mother and hold fast to his wife, and the two shall become one flesh'? So they are no longer two but one flesh. What therefore God has joined together, let not man separate."
~Matthew 19:4-6 ESV

It was raining really hard one day when I had to take my ninety-something grandma to the doctor. I pulled up as close as I could to the door in order to get her in without her getting soaked to the skin. After getting her inside, going to park the car, and running back inside, we sat down to wait our turn. We'd been waiting about thirty minutes when a couple easily in their eighties, struggled to get in the door. A woman near the door rushed over to help them. Once inside, you couldn't help but notice that both of them were soaking wet. She was barely able to walk, yet she was pushing his wheelchair, and had pushed it from the parking space to the door…after struggling to get him from the car into the chair…in the pouring down rain."
"After checking in at the desk, the woman took some tissues from the box on the table and started drying her husband's face and head. He looked up at her, smiled, then took one of the tissues from her and reached up to do the same for her."
"Call me rude…call nearly everyone in the waiting room

rude, but we couldn't help but watch the two of them in awe. Thankfully it didn't take more than a few seconds for several of us to stop watching and actually help by getting a couple of towels for them to use to dry themselves off." "I know nearly everyone in our small-ish community, but I didn't know them. You can be sure, however, that I will never forget them. Nearly fifteen years later I can still see their faces, their gentle smiles, the way he reached up to dry her face, the soft, "Thank you, honey," he said two or three times. I will never forget them because I know without a doubt God sent them to me and to everyone else in that waiting room to remind us what love through the years looks like. What it feels like. What it is." If this elderly couple had never experienced a hardship, heartache, or hard time, until whatever happened to put the man in a wheelchair, I would be shocked. Loving devotion like theirs didn't happen overnight, and it didn't happen because they'd lived a life of privilege and ease. The loving devotion this couple had for one another happened over the passing of years spent encouraging one another, caring for one another, comforting one another, sharing with one another, resolving conflicts with one another, and drawing near to God with one another. God desires and expects the same in your marriage. Will you give God this desire? Will you meet his expectations for your marriage?

Prayer

God, thank you for my husband/wife. Thank you for bringing us together and thank you for giving us your Word and the example of couples who are older and farther along in their marriage journey. Help us look to both of these for strength and guidance. Help us always turn to each other and give each other the very best of ourselves. In Jesus' name, amen.

Week Seven: Through The Years

TASK 1
Think of some couples you know who have been married at least twenty years. Ask them to share their thoughts on why their marriage works

___

Souls in Harmony

TASK 2 WHAT DO YOU CONSIDER THE STRONG POINTS OF YOUR MARRIAGE TO BE? THE WEAK POINTS? DISCUSS THESE THINGS AND DECIDE WHAT YOU WILL DO TO MAKE THE STRONG POINTS STRONGER AND TURN THE WEAKNESSES INTO STRENGTHS OR DO AWAY WITH THEM ALTOGETHER.

Week Seven: Through The Years

TASK 3

TALK ABOUT THE ACCOMPLISHMENTS YOU'VE MADE AS A COUPLE AND INDIVIDUALLY SINCE YOU'VE BEEN MARRIED. HOW HAS WORKING TOGETHER AS A COUPLE MADE THESE THINGS POSSIBLE—EVEN YOUR INDIVIDUAL ACCOMPLISHMENTS?

TASK 4
WHAT GOALS DO YOU HAVE FOR YOUR MARRIAGE? WHAT IS YOUR PLAN FOR ACCOMPLISHING THEM?

Week Seven: Through The Years

Week Eight: I Choose Happy

And the peace of God, which surpasses all understanding, will guard your hearts and your minds in Christ Jesus. ~Philippians 4:7 ESV

There are countless verses that could be used to draw your attention to this week's focus on happiness. I chose this one, though, because of the words, "…surpasses all…" and "…will guard….". There is power in the word 'all'. It means everything. Nothing left out. No exceptions. As for the words, 'will guard', that makes me feel safe and secure. They are like a wall of protection against anything that might try to hurt me. To disrupt or destroy my peace. We need all of these things in our marriages. We need to be at peace—to know without a doubt—that nothing is going to come between us and our spouse. No one or nothing will be able to cause us to break the vows we spoke to each other and to God. No exceptions. We also need to know that there is only once source for this peace, which is Jesus. And because of that, we need to make Jesus the core and the outer covering for our marriage. We need to let the peace of Jesus guard our hearts and minds against:

- Petty arguments
- Resentment and unforgiveness
- Suspicion
- Lust

- Greed
- Dishonesty
- Selfishness
- Putting other people and things higher on the priority list than our marriage
- Letting other people into our marriage (parents, friends, co-workers)
- Disrespect
- Taking our spouse for granted
- Poor self-esteem
- Looking elsewhere for validation and satisfaction (food, gambling, sports, work, money, your children, material possessions, hobbies, friends, members of theopposite sex)

Marriage is hard work, but it comes with a unique set of blessings and privileges you won't get from anything or anyone else. Marriage is also an analogy God wants us to live each and every day of our lives in order that we might better understand his love and devotion for the Church.

This week is meant to be a week of refreshing. Refresh your marriage by shaking out all the peace-robbers and sending them on their way, and replace them with the peace of Jesus Christ that comes by putting him first in your life and in the life of your marriage.

Prayer

God, guard my body, heart, and mind. Keep it pure and focused on my marriage and do the same for my spouse. God, thank you for my marriage and for the peace you offer that allows us to experience your presence in our hearts and in our home. In the name of Jesus, amen.

Week Eight: I Choose Happy

TASK 1

TAKE ANOTHER LOOK AT THE LIST OF THINGS THAT TRY TO STEAL THE PEACE OUT OF OUR MARRIAGES. NEXT TO EACH ONE, WRITE DOWN SOMETHING YOU WILL DO TO DELIBERATELY REMOVE IT FROM YOUR MARRIAGE.

TASK 2

SPEND SOME TIME EACH DAY THIS WEEK PRAYING WITH YOUR SPOUSE FOR YOUR MARRIAGE.

_____
_____
_____
_____
_____
_____
_____
_____
_____
_____
_____
_____
_____
_____
_____
_____
_____
_____
_____

Week Eight: I Choose Happy

TASK 3

What is one thing you would like your spouse to do to better guard your marriage? Share your answers with each other and decide what you can and will do to honor this request.

_____
_____
_____
_____
_____
_____
_____
_____
_____
_____
_____
_____
_____
_____
_____
_____
_____
_____
_____
_____
_____

Souls in Harmony

Week Nine: Because God Wants Me To

Submitting to one another out of reverence for Christ. ~Ephesians 5:21 ESV

This week we're going to look closely at one of the most controversial matters in a marriage—submission. And I'm not talking about marriages among non-believers. I'm talking about marriages among Christians. Seems that a lot of Christian couples have no problem agreeing with what God has to say about greed, purity, giving, praying, and a bunch of other things. But when it comes to submission, well, that's just won't work for us (or so they say).

The truth of the matter is that submission does 'work'. It works very well. And the reason it works so well is because submission was designed by God.

The word 'submission' has two different meanings. One: to acknowledge and yield to authority. Two: to present an idea or proposal for consideration of acceptance. It's definition number one that people—primarily wives—have a problem with. They feel that yielding to authority is demeaning and a declaration of inadequacy and worth, but that's simply not true.

In a Christian marriage, the authority wives are submitting to isn't their husband's. They are submitting to God's authority.

Besides, the wife isn't the only one doing the submitting. Husband's have the responsibility to submit to God's authority, too, and then they have the added responsibility of mirroring that authority in your marriage and in your home.

Do you understand what this means? It means that when a husband submits to God by loving their wives as Christ loves the Church, his wife is going to be treated loved, honored, respected, and cherished. He's not going to ask anything of her that he wouldn't ask of himself. Take a minute to let that sink in. Is there any part of that a wife should object to?

Submission done God's way also links back to the second definition. Wives, submission doesn't reduce you to being a mute slave. No way! Again—that's not what submission is. Submission is communicating, sharing, discussing, asking, telling, agreeing, disagreeing, and in marriage, even arguing from time to time, BUT, when all is said and done, the husband is to have the final say and his wife is to respect and honor what he says.

I could keep writing for quite some time on the subject, but I won't. Instead, I want you to focus on what God has to say. Spend time this week reading, talking about, and praying about submission in your marriage. Oh, and one more thing…make submission a real thing in your marriage and then enjoy the blessings of what it does for your relationship. I promise. No… God promises.

Prayer

LORD, mold our hearts and minds to your way of thinking and your design for marriage. Help me love my wife as you love the Church. Help me put her needs and the needs of my family in the forefront of my mind. And LORD, let me trust my husband to always have my best interest at heart. Don't let me stand in his way of obeying you by refusing to let him be the head of our household. Let ours be a marriage and household of faith and obedience. In Jesus' name, amen.

Week Nine: Because God Wants Me To

TASK 1

READ EACH OF THE FOLLOWING VERSES. IF POSSIBLE, JUST FOCUS ON ONE OF THEM EACH DAY THIS WEEK. SHARE YOUR HONEST THOUGHTS AND FEELINGS ON WHAT IT SAYS. TALK ABOUT HOW YOUR MARRIAGE WOULD BE DIFFERENT IF YOU LIVED OUT THESE COMMANDS FROM GOD.

Now as the church submits to Christ, so also wives should submit in everything to their husbands. ~Ephesians 5:24 ESV

_____
_____
_____
_____
_____
_____
_____

Husbands, love your wives, as Christ loved the church and gave himself up for her… ~Ephesians 5:25 ESV

_____
_____
_____
_____
_____
_____
_____

For this is how the holy women who hoped in God used to adorn themselves, by submitting to their own husbands, as Sarah obeyed Abraham, calling him lord. And you are her children, if you do good and do not fear anything that is frightening. ~1st Peter 3:5-6 ESV

_____
_____
_____
_____
_____
_____
_____

Wives, submit to your husbands, as is fitting in the Lord. `Colossians 3:18 ESV

_____
_____
_____
_____
_____
_____
_____

Week Nine: Because God Wants Me To

Likewise, wives, be subject to your own husbands, so that even if some do not obey the word, they may be won without a word by the conduct of their wives… ~1st Peter 3:1 ESV

Agree with God, and be at peace; thereby good will come to you. ~Job 22:21 ESV

Let every person be subject to the governing authorities. For there is no authority except from God, and those that exist have been instituted by God. ~Romans 13:1 ESV

Souls in Harmony

TASK 2

HUSBANDS: GENTLY, BUT HONESTLY TELL YOUR WIFE WHAT YOU NEED FROM HER TO FEEL MORE LIKE THE HEAD OF YOUR HOUSEHOLD.

_____
_____
_____
_____
_____
_____
_____
_____
_____
_____
_____
_____
_____
_____
_____
_____

Week Nine: Because God Wants Me To

TASK 3

WIVES: GENTLY, BUT HONESTLY TELL YOUR HUSBAND ABOUT ANY RESERVATIONS OR FEARS YOU HAVE ABOUT BEING SUBMISSIVE. TELL HIM WHAT YOU NEED FROM HIM TO RESPECT AND HONOR HIS POSITION AS THE HEAD OF YOUR HOUSEHOLD.

_____
_____
_____
_____
_____
_____
_____
_____
_____
_____
_____
_____
_____
_____
_____
_____
_____
_____
_____
_____

Week Ten: A Healthy Dose of Fear

The end of the matter; all has been heard. Fear God and keep his commandments, for this is the whole duty of man. ~Ecclesiastes 12:13 ESV

How many times have you wives said, "Wait until your dad gets home."? Or how many times did you hear that same warning come from your own mother's mouth? And mind you, both you and she said it in a tone of voice dripping with doom and peril. But why? What's so bad about dad? He loves you, you love him…what's the problem? There is no problem with Dad. And you're right—Dads do love us. He also works hard for us (his family). He's not bad at all. In fact, Dad is pretty darn great. So again, why all the doom and gloom? The problem that sparked the warning of impending doom is because of something you or your child said or did—depending on the situation. Something that was clearly a line-crossing act of disobedience. When that happens, it's Dad's job to make sure his kids suffer the consequences of their actions. The way this is (was) supposed to work is that when Dad gets home, he listens to Mom recount the event that lead to the 'wait until…' warning, calls his child into the room, tells him/her he knows what happened, asks what they have to say about the situation, then pronounces and carries out an appropriate punishment. The child is scared they aren't going to like the consequences they know are coming. But it's the consequences that frighten them—not Dad or Mom. Dad and Mom love them too much to hold a grudge or to be too harsh and unfair. But a child also understands the value of staying in their parents' good graces, i.e. being obedient. The same thing is true in our relationship with God. He disciplines and punishes us when we cross the boundary lines of morality and doctrine he has given. But he never withholds his love. He does, however, want us to be fearful of the consequences for testing that love. He wants us to realize and respect how deeply offended he gets when we disobey and break our promise to give him first place in our lives. "I agree—but what does that have to do with my marriage?" you ask. Good question. Now here's the answer… You need to be fearful FOR your marriage. You need to understand that Satan is dead-set, full-on, determined to undermine and destroy as many marriages as he possibly can. You also need to understand that your marriage is on his radar—that no matter how solid you think you are, no matter now much you love each other, no matter how many years you've been married or how many difficult times you've survived together, your marriage is in danger of being destroyed by Satan. Okay, now that I've painted such a beautiful picture for you, let's talk about how you need to be fearful. Fearing for your marriage should be done in the same way God wants you to fear him.

- Invest your whole self in your marriage—just like God wants all of you in your relationship with him.
- Refuse to let doubt, resentment, worry, suspicion, and selfishness intrude in your marriage. Just like 2nd Corinthians 10:5 tells us to take every thought captive and give it to Christ, take every thought you have about your marriage captive and put it through the filter of Christ's definition of love.

- Putting other people and things higher on the priority list than our marriage
- Obey Jesus' command to not let any man (or woman) separate the union between a husband and wife. Don't put your kids, grandkids, friends, extended family, co-workers, boss, or anyone else in front of your husband. God is to be first place in our lives, and our spouses, second.
- Keep yourself sexually pure. This includes filtering the books you read, the movies/television you watch, the websites you visit, the conversations you have with the opposite sex, and the clothes you wear.
- Obey the Golden Rule to treat your spouse the way you want to be treated.
- Just like we need to spend time daily talking to God, listening to God, and worshipping God, we need to spend time daily talking, listening to, and admiring our spouse.
- Fearing for your marriage is healthy. When you fear for your marriage, you greatly reduce the chances of taking it for granted, which is exactly what Satan wants you to do.

Prayer

God, open my eyes to the dangers around me—the things and people that pose a threat to my marriage. Give me the energy and desire to fight hard for my marriage and to have a fearful respect of what can happen when we take each other for granted. Thank you for my husband/wife. Help me show him/her how very much I love him/her. In Jesus' name, amen.

TASK 1
WHAT ARE YOUR THOUGHTS AND FEELINGS ABOUT THE TERM, 'FEAR FOR YOUR MARRIAGE'?

_____
_____
_____
_____
_____
_____
_____
_____
_____
_____
_____
_____
_____
_____
_____
_____
_____
_____
_____
_____

Souls in Harmony

TASK 2 HOW HAVE YOU BEEN TAKING YOUR MARRIAGE FOR GRANTED? CONFESS THESE THINGS TO GOD, ASK HIS FORGIVENESS, AND ASK FOR STRENGTH AND A HEART FULL OF DESIRE TO DO BETTER..

_____
_____
_____
_____
_____
_____
_____
_____
_____
_____
_____
_____
_____
_____
_____
_____
_____

Week Ten: A Healthy Dose of Fear

TASK 3 — MAKE A LIST OF SOME THINGS YOU CAN DO TO BETTER PROTECT YOUR MARRIAGE AND START DOING THEM TODAY.

_____
_____
_____
_____
_____
_____
_____
_____
_____
_____
_____
_____
_____
_____
_____
_____
_____
_____
_____
_____

Week Eleven: You'll Shoot Your Eye Out

If your right eye causes you to stumble, gouge it out and throw it away. It is better for you to lose one part of your body than for your whole body to be thrown into hell. ~Matthew 5:29 ESV

Be honest—when you read the title to this week's devotion, did you say it (or think it) in that same gravelly, gruff Santa Claus voice in the movie, "A Christmas Story"? You know the story, don't you? Ralphie wants a Red Rider BB gun for Christmas. He wants it so bad he can hardly stand it. His mom says, no—that he'll shoot his eye out. So he decides to go out on a limb and ask Santa. He's dubious enough about whether or not Santa is real, but hey, it couldn't hurt to ask, right? Wrong. Santa, in a most loving, endearing attitude (not) doesn't blink an eyelash before responding to Ralphie's request with, "You'll shoot your eye out, kid.".

If you've seen the movie you know Ralphie's dad, who you think would be the last person to empathize with his son, decides to grant Ralphie's Christmas wish by making sure there's a Red Rider BB gun under the tree on Christmas morning. Ralphie is ecstatic! He can't wait to get outside in the freezing cold weather for some target practice, where almost immediately, he shoots his eye out. Well, sort of. The bb ricochets back and hits and breaks Ralphie's glasses.

In Ralphie's case, putting his eye out was not a good thing. But this week's verse tells us that's exactly what we need to do if it comes down to that or putting our salvation in jeopardy. But is that really what Jesus is saying…literally?

The question we want to address this week is: How can you protect your marriage against lust? In order to answer that question, we need to fully understand what lust is. Jesus says in this verse that lust is looking at 'her' (another woman) in such a way that you think about how desirable she is. This doesn't mean a man should never see a woman and be able to say things like, "She's pretty." "That's a nice dress. I think it would look good on you, honey." Or "I admire the way she conducts herself in the office." Lust is looking at her and thinking you'd like to get to know her better, admire her figure, fantasize about her, or go out of your way to see or talk to her.

See the difference? But wait—there's more. While Jesus is speaking specifically of a male/female attraction, there are a lot of other things that can soil the purity of your marriage. The 'her' in this verse could be several different things, and you would do well to realize that. As husbands and wives, we need to be diligent in keeping our relationship pure. We need to protect our physical and emotional vision in order to save both our marriage and our souls.

As you think about what this means, ask yourselves this question: What actions on the part of your husband or wife would make you feel betrayed?
- Sexual infidelity?
- Flirting with someone?
- Dressing suggestively when mingling with members of the

Souls in Harmony

opposite sex?
- Hiding money or lying about the amount of money being spent?
- Talking about you and/or your marriage behind your back?
- Disrespecting you in front of your children, or anyone else?
- Making fun of or being dismissive of your feelings and concerns.

While sexual purity is a definite must in marriage, lust is about a lot more than 'just' sex. Lust is having a strong desire for anything to the point of throwing away what you have in order to get it. Don't throw your marriage away because of lust. Just don't.

Prayer

God, keep us pure in heart, mind, soul, and body. Help us be loyal, faithful, and honest to you and to each other. In Jesus' name, amen.

TASK 1
WHAT THING(S) DO YOU LUST AFTER... OR ARE YOU MOST TEMPTED TO LUST AFTER?

_____
_____
_____
_____
_____
_____
_____
_____
_____
_____
_____
_____
_____
_____
_____
_____
_____
_____
_____
_____
_____
_____
_____
_____

TASK 2

WHAT STEPS ARE YOU TAKING TO KEEP THESE THINGS FROM HARMING YOUR MARRIAGE?

_____
_____
_____
_____
_____
_____
_____
_____
_____
_____
_____
_____
_____
_____
_____
_____
_____
_____
_____
_____

Week Eleven: You'll Shoot Your Eye Out

TASK 3
WHAT ARE SOME PRACTICAL STEPS YOU CAN (AND WILL) TAKE TO PREVENT THE TEMPTATION OF LUST?

_____
_____
_____
_____
_____
_____
_____
_____
_____
_____
_____
_____
_____
_____
_____
_____
_____
_____
_____

Week Twelve: Hold My Hand...Not a Grudge

Let all bitterness and wrath and anger and clamor and slander be put away from you, along with all malice. Be kind to one another, tenderhearted, forgiving one another, as God in Christ forgave you. ~Ephesians 4:31-32 ESV

David had two small children and an ex-wife who left and never looked back—not even to see her children. So when he met Valerie, he saw in her the possibility for a second chance at love, as well as someone to love and nurture his children in mother-like fashion. Valerie was all-in, but because this was her first marriage, she expressed to David that she would like to add to their family—to have at least one child together. He agreed with a smile on his face...and a lie in his heart.

Afraid Valerie would end the relationship, David decided not to tell Valerie he'd had a vasectomy after his youngest child was born. Instead, he decided to 'try' for a baby, console Valerie through the pain of infertility, and hope he could convince her that his two children were God's way of blessing her with a family.

Long story short, after nearly three heart-breaking years of not getting pregnant, Valerie found out the truth. She was heartbroken and angry. Every ounce of trust she had was gone. The foundation of lies the marriage was built on crumbled, and it took years of intense Godly counseling, a lot of prayer, humility, and mega-doses of forgiveness to rebuild their marriage on a more secure foundation. There were more than a few times Valerie wanted to walk away, and quite honestly, nearly ever felt she was justified in doing so. But she always came back to this week's verse. When someone is truly sorry and repentant, as Christians, we have no choice but to forgive, because we have been called to forgive in the same way God forgives us.

Hopefully your marriage will never be put to such a test as this, but it doesn't have to be in order for unforgiveness to threaten its stability. Having a heart of unforgiveness over toothpaste tubes and toilet seats is just as dangerous, so remember—bitterness and unforgiveness have no place in your marriage.

Prayer

Father in heaven, give me the ability to forgive in the same way you forgive. LORD, it's not easy. I've been hurt. I feel disrespected and unappreciated. But haven't I made you feel the same, yet you forgive me when I ask you? Let me be like you by giving me the gift of freedom tha comes with forgiveness. In your son's name, I pray, amen.

TASK 1   WHAT GRUDGES ARE YOU HOLDING AGAINST YOUR SPOUSE? WHY?

_____
_____
_____
_____
_____
_____
_____
_____
_____
_____
_____
_____
_____
_____
_____
_____
_____
_____

Week Twelve: Hold My Hand…Not a Grudge

TASK 2
SPEND SOME TIME IN PRAYER—JUST YOU AND GOD. ASK GOD TO SOFTEN YOUR HEART TOWARD YOUR SPOUSE.

TASK 3

FORGIVE YOUR SPOUSE. VERBALLY EXPRESS YOUR FORGIVENESS—EVEN IF THEY DON'T EVEN REALIZE YOU WERE HOLDING A GRUDGE.

_____
_____
_____
_____
_____
_____
_____
_____
_____
_____
_____
_____
_____
_____
_____
_____
_____
_____
_____

Week Twelve: Hold My Hand…Not a Grudge

Week Thirteen: Praise God from Whom All Blessings of Marriage Flow

O Lord, you are my God; I will exalt you; I will praise your name, for you have done wonderful things, plans formed of old, faithful and sure. ~Isaiah 25:1 ESV

Have you ever heard someone whose tech savviness is elementary at best, say something like, "I've got this fancy phone, but I really don't know what to do with it."? Or have you ever been trying to pay for your lunch at the fast-food counter and the person trying to operate the cash register/computer was having a first-day-on-the-job-so-I-don't-have-a-clue kind of day? Or maybe you've been 'lucky' enough to go through your child's 6th grade year with them having a music major as a math teacher because they couldn't find a math teacher to fill the position?

There's a glaring similarity in all three situations. Do you see it? In all three situations, potential isn't being realized. The phone, the new employee, and the teacher aren't living up to their potential because they are out of their element. They are trying to do something without being properly or thoroughly equipped.

Souls in Harmony

The same can be said about you and your spouse if you are trying to be half of a husband/wife team without being a whole person first. Without fulfilling your primary purpose for being here in the first place, which is to worship God.

When we spend time each and every day worshipping the One who created us…who loves us…who provides for us…who saved us, we can't help but be better. Worship given to God comes back to us in the form of peace, contentment, joy, and a love meant to be shared. And who better to share it with than the one you are married to?

You've heard the saying, "Happy wife…happy life", haven't you? Well the same goes for husbands, too. And the best way to make your spouse happy is to be truly happy yourself…happy in the LORD.

Prayer

LORD, We praise you for your holiness, for salvation, and for one another. Amen.

PART 1 — DO YOU WORSHIP GOD OUTSIDE OF CORPORATE WORSHIP AT CHURCH? HOW? HOW OFTEN?

_____
_____
_____
_____
_____
_____
_____
_____
_____
_____
_____
_____
_____
_____
_____
_____
_____
_____
_____

PART 2 — DO YOU AND YOUR SPOUSE WORSHIP TOGETHER? PRAY TOGETHER?

_____
_____
_____
_____
_____
_____
_____
_____
_____
_____
_____
_____
_____
_____
_____
_____
_____
_____
_____
_____
_____
_____

Week Thirteen: Praise God from Whom All Blessings of Marriage Flow

PART 3 SPEND SOME TIME THIS WEEK WORSHIPPING GOD TOGETHER BY THANKING GOD FOR THE SPECIFIC BLESSINGS YOU HAVE EXPERIENCED IN YOUR MARRIAGE.

_____
_____
_____
_____
_____
_____
_____
_____
_____
_____
_____
_____
_____
_____
_____
_____
_____
_____
_____
_____

PART 4 SPEND SOME TIME LISTENING TO YOUR FAVORITE PRAISE AND WORSHIP SONGS/HYMNS AND SHARING YOUR FAVORITE BIBLE VERSES WITH EACH OTHER.

___

Week Thirteen: Praise God from Whom All Blessings of Marriage Flow

Week Fourteen: The Couple That Prays and Plays Together Stays Together

And let us consider how to stir up one another to love and good works. ~Hebrews 10:24 ESV

The word 'love' is one of the most over-used and mis-used words in the English language. I mean, seriously, do we really love pizza? The feel of new socks on our feet? The smell of homemade bread in the over? A good mystery book? Sure those things are yummy, cozy feeling, and enjoyable, but is love really involved? Love is all those things Paul tells us in 1st Corinthians 13. Patient. Kind. Humble. Selfless. Forgiving…and so on. You can't do any of those things with pizza, socks, bread, or a book because you can't interact with any of those things. They are just objects—not people. But you can do those things for and with your spouse. Actually, you need to be doing those things together in order to have the relationship you crave and God desires.

In order for there to be genuine love, there has to be a deep through and through connection. Love based on looks, money, or anything else that offers us satisfaction isn't love. That's why I really dislike the terms 'falling in love' and 'falling out of love'. You don't fall in love. You choose to love. Love is not an event.

Souls in Harmony

It's a conscious and deliberate choice of response and behavior. The same is true about falling out of love. You don't fall out of love. You choose not to love. You choose to disrespect, be selfish, break promises—to respond and behave in a way that doesn't include love.

You may or may not already know this, but your 20-something looks and figure aren't going to follow you into your forties and beyond. Your hair is going to gray or disappear altogether. Your skin is going to go from smooth to…not. The day is coming when you won't need or want sex several times a week. The busy-ness and noise of raising kids is going to level off and then drive off with the clunker cars they (the kids take to college); leaving just the two of you. You will be each other's conversation partner, date, and caregiver. When these things happen, and again, they are going to happen, you want to know beyond a shadow of a doubt that you can depend on each other, confide in each other, and enjoy one anthother.

This week's verse is meant to remind you to be deliberate and intentional in developing that through and through kind of connection in your marriage. Look and love beyond the physical. Work toward developing a deeper spiritual and emotional connection that will solidify your love. Pray together. Read God's Word together. Worship together. Laugh together. Play together. Serve others together. Dream about a future of togetherness and ask God to bless you in your efforts to truly be one in heart, body, and mind with him.

Prayer

God, keep the desire for us to take our marriage to a deeper level at the forefront of our minds. Help us always look for ways to draw closer to you…together. Amen.

Week Fourteen: The Couple That Prays and Plays Together Stays Together

TASK 1
MAKE A LIST OF ACTIVITIES YOU WOULD LIKE TO DO WITH YOUR SPOUSE. TRY YOUR BEST TO DO AT LEAST ONE OF THESE EACH WEEK.

Souls in Harmony

TASK 2

HOW OFTEN DO YOU PRAY TOGETHER? ARE YOU COMFORTABLE DOING SO? IF NOT, WHY?

_____
_____
_____
_____
_____
_____
_____
_____
_____
_____
_____
_____
_____
_____
_____
_____

Week Fourteen: The Couple That Prays and Plays Together Stays Together

TASK 3

WHAT 'GOD QUESTIONS' DO YOU HAVE? FOR EXAMPLE, WHAT HAPPENS WHEN WE DIE, WILL WE KNOW WE WERE MARRIED WHEN WE GET TO HEAVEN, AND THINGS LIKE THAT. TALK ABOUT THESE THINGS WITH YOUR SPOUSE AND SPEND SOME TIME SEARCHING THE BIBLE FOR ANSWERS TO THESE QUESTIONS.

FYI: www.openbible.info is a great resource for doing this.

_____
_____
_____
_____
_____
_____
_____
_____
_____
_____
_____
_____
_____
_____

Souls in Harmony

Week Fifteen: It's the Thought That Counts

So then let us pursue what makes for peace and for mutual upbuilding. ~Romans 14:19 ESV

When Rhonda came home from an extended stay in the hospital, she was overwhelmed by the efforts of her husband to have the house tidy and clean, the laundry washed, folded, and put away, fresh sheets on the bed, and tried to fill the pantry with all her favorite foods. It didn't bother her one bit that he'd used so much fabric softener that the towels were a bit gummy or that he'd bought two bottles of conditioner for her hair instead of both shampoo and conditioner.

Joni had dropped more than a few hints about wanting a new sewing machine for Christmas. Neither Will nor the kids took the bait, though. Instead, Will listened to their six year-old who swore up and down that Mom (Joni) had her heart seat on some fuzzy pj's and slippers. Knowing how cold-natured his wife is… Joni smiled, oohed, and awed over the gift; saying it was just what she'd been hoping for.

Gwynn knew her husband would be exhausted after working out of town for the past two weeks. He would barely get home on Friday afternoon before their houseful of company would arrive for her youngest sister's wedding. She wanted to do anything and everything she could to make his homecoming as pleasant and seamless as possible, she took the time to mow the lawn and make sure everything was neatly trimmed and weeded. Mowing was no problem—she mowed the lawn about half the time anyway. Weeding the flowerbeds was also her normal responsibility. It was the weed eater that was about as alien to her as snow in July. It had always intimidated her, so she'd never bothered to learn how to use it. But how hard could it be? Famous last words, as they say. Gwynn had barely made it down one side of the sidewalk before the spool of cutting string was a wadded-up mess. There was no way she could fix that and master the weed eater, so she put it away and finished the old-fashioned way…with the clippers.

When she finally 'came clean' to Will (after the wedding festivities were over and their company had gone home), the perfectionist in him wanted to get angry, but he couldn't. Knowing how hard Gwynn had worked to lessen his load despite the fact that she had plenty to do to get ready for their company and the wedding was a huge and sacrificial labor of love and he wasn't about to make her think he saw it as anything less than that.

We humans have a need and desire to with someone—to love and be loved. But just like an old 45 (vinyl record for those of you who don't know what an 'old 45 is), we have a flipside. And the flipside of our need to love and be loved is our tendencies to be selfish and self-preserving. The stark contrast of these two natural (inborn) tendencies can cause both internal and external conflicts that can easily spill over into your marriage if you aren't careful.

It takes a conscious effort on your part (you, as in both of you) to make sure you pursue those things that encourage and build your spouse up and make your marriage a place of peace and contentment.

Souls in Harmony

When God realized it wasn't good for man to be alone (Genesis 2:18), he created Eve.

Take a minute to re-read that last statement. God didn't want Adam to be alone, so he created Eve. He created Eve so they could be mutually uplifting and useful to each other. So they could live a more peaceful and contented life.

Do you and your spouse compliment each other? Do you go out of your way to make each other's lives easier? More pleasant? If so, you are undoubtedly experiencing God's continued blessings on your marriage. If not, why aren't you?

Prayer

LORD, help me be conscious of making my husband/wife feel special. Give me eyes that see and hands that are capable of making their life easier and less busy. Bless us with the joy that comes from blessing each other. In your son's name I pray, amen.

TASK 1

What are some things your spouse could do to make your life easier? Spend some time sharing your 'list'. Each of you should then choose at least two of these things and do them.

_____
_____
_____
_____
_____
_____
_____
_____
_____
_____
_____
_____
_____
_____
_____
_____
_____
_____
_____
_____

TASK 2

IS THERE SOMETHING YOUR SPOUSE DOES 'FOR YOU' THAT YOU WISH HE/SHE WOULDN'T DO—SOMETHING THAT ACTUALLY MAKES LIFE MORE COMPLICATED OR BUSY? BE GENTLY HONEST IN SHARING THIS INFORMATION WITH EACH OTHER AND COME TO A MUTUAL AGREEMENT ON HOW TO HANDLE THE SITUATION POSITIVELY.

TASK 3: BEGINNING THIS WEEK, TAKE THE TIME TO BUILD YOUR SPOUSE UP IN A SPECIAL WAY AT LEAST ONCE A WEEK.

Some suggestions for what you can do include: sending a text 'love note', taking lunch to the office and eating together, giving them an hour 'off' to do whatever they want to do, surprising them with flowers, a warm cinnamon roll, a new book, getting the car detailed, a candlelight dinner after the kids go to bed, watching their favorite movie with them, treating them to a manicure (her) or hockey game with a friend (him)…you get the picture.

___

___

___

___

___

___

___

___

___

___

___

___

___

___

Souls in Harmony

Week Sixteen: Marriage Is...

It is better to live in a corner of the housetop than in a house shared with a quarrelsome wife. ~Proverbs 21:9 ESV

This week's verse has been used by more than a few husbands to tease their wives. Teasing or not, there's a lot of truth in these twenty words. But then why wouldn't there be? It's the Bible!

This week's devotion is meant to draw you more deeply into the Bible. By looking more intently at what the Bible has to say about marriage, the roles of husbands and wives, and about making God the nucleus as well as the covering of your marriage. So that's what you're going to do. Take time each day to read and re-read the following verses. Pray individually and as a couple that you can be the husband and wife God is calling you to be.

Let marriage be held in honor among all, and let the marriage bed be undefiled, for God will judge the sexually immoral and adulterous. ~Hebrews 13:4 ESV

Stay faithful to your spouse. Keep your relationships with members of the opposite sex at a very safe distance. These relationships need to be very open and simple, shared with your spouse, and never engage in conversations that could be construed as anything other than Christian brotherhood and friendship or work-related.

Stay faithful to your spouse by refusing to cave to the temptations of pornography, sexually explicit movies or television, sexually-charged jokes, or flirting.

Stay faithful to your spouse by refusing to go places that might cause you to lust or cause your husband or wife to feel betrayed or disrespected.

Therefore a man shall leave his father and his mother and hold fast to his wife, and they shall become one flesh. ~Genesis 2:24 ESV

Guard your marriage against interference from extended family members and friends. Let your family and friends know you are a united team of two as one. Don't talk negatively about each other to your family or friends. Don't share your disagreements and arguments between you and your spouse with family and friends. Don't let family and friends take priority over your marriage and your own family.

Guard your marriage against the pressures of giving more of yourself to your job than you give to your marriage and family. Learn to say no.

Likewise, husbands, live with your wives in an understanding way, showing honor to the woman as the weaker vessel, since they are heirs with you of the grace of life, so that your prayers may not be hindered. ~1st Peter 3:7 ESV

Treat each other with respect. Recognize and 'own' the differences between men and women. This is not a bad thing—it's a God thing. Two becoming one means you compliment each other's strengths and work together to bring strength to your weaknesses.

Wives, submit to your husbands, as is fitting in the Lord. Husbands, love your wives, and do not be harsh with them. ~Colossians 3:18-19 ESV

Week nine hopefully gave you a fresh and Godly perspective on what submission is and isn't, but it never hurts to be reminded of something God views as important and vital to a marriage as the balance of submission and leadership. Mutual respect and selflessness. Compromise and cooperation.

Guard your marriage by submitting to God first. When both of you submit to God first, everything else will fall into place. Husbands will never ask anything of their wives they wouldn't do themselves and they lead out of a desire to please both God and their wives.

Wives, on the other hand, will trust their husbands to bring them good, rather than harm. Their husband's love for God will be evident in all they do; giving them the confidence that God is the head of their marriage, so everything will work for their good.

What therefore God has joined together, let not man separate. ~Mark 10:9 ESV

Guard your marriage against infidelity by making and keeping firm boundaries for relationships with members of the opposite sex in place.

Guard your marriage against infidelity by closely monitoring and limiting content that comes into your home and across your devices.

Guard your marriage against divisions and separations caused by intrusions by other people (extended family members, children/step-children, ex-spouses).

Guard your marriage against separations by keeping a proper perspective on time spent at work, time spent with friend, time spent serving and ministering to others, and on hobbies and outside interests.

When a man is newly married, he shall not go out with the army or be liable for any other public duty. He shall be free at home one year to be happy with his wife whom he has taken. ~Deuteronomy

Week Sixteen: Marriage Is…

24:5 ESV

Guard your marriage by making a conscious and intentional effort to really know the person you are married to. Know them well enough to read their moods, anticipate their needs and wants, how to effectively communicate with them, when to give them their space, and when to be their safe landing.
You're right—these things aren't easy to learn about a person. It takes time and energy…and lots of it. Don't worry, though. You've got a lifetime to work on it.

It is better to live in a desert land than with a quarrelsome and fretful woman. ~Proverbs 21:9 ESV

—

A quarrelsome wife is like the dripping of a leaky roof in a rainstorm… ~Proverbs 27:15 NIV

Guard your marriage by talking instead of lecturing, disagreeing instead of arguing, listening instead of ignoring, planning instead of plotting, sharing instead of hiding, encouraging instead of discouraging.

An excellent wife who can find? She is far more precious than jewels. The heart of her husband trusts in her, and he will have no lack of gain. She does him good, and not harm, all the days of her life. ~Proverbs 31:10-12 ESV

—

The wisest of women builds her house, but folly with her own hands tears it down. ~Proverbs 14:1

Although these verses describe the ideal wife, husbands would do well to possess these same traits. An excellent husband or excellent wife oozes with Godly grace and integrity. He or she lives to bring God glory and to make his/her spouse shine. Does this describe your marriage?

Above all, keep loving one another earnestly, since love covers a multitude of sins. ~1st Peter 4:8 ESV

It really is that simple…love one another earnestly. Deeply. Sincerely. With forever as your goal.

PRAYER

God, help us take these words of yours to heart and make them the mantras of our marriage. In the name of Jesus, amen.

# Week Seventeen: When Mr. Satan Knocks

And give no opportunity to the devil. ~Ephesians 4:27

There's a song we used to sing in children's church way back when, that went like this: When Mr. Satan knocks at my heart's door and says, "May I come in?" I say, "NO! NO! For Jesus loves me so and he took away my sin." So he turns around and runs away; I hope he goes and stays away. When Mr. Satan knocks at my heart's door, I just say, "No! No! No!".

Our Sunday school teachers and children's church teachers weren't afraid to tell us about Satan. They believed, as do I, that we need to be very aware of who he is and what he is capable of. But that doesn't seem to be the case in most churches these days. Far too many churches choose instead, to focus on a prosperity gospel, a church experience built around an entertainment-style praise band, and the Jesus who would never let anything bad happen to us.

A lot of preachers rarely open their Bible when preaching a sermon. Instead, they choose to talk about social issues from a politically correct point of view and with the intention of making everyone comfortable with who they are with no pressure to change and grow to be more like Jesus. Satan and hell are never talked about. They should be.

Souls in Harmony

Satan is a voracious opponent to your faith and your marriage. But just like athletic coaches spend time studying their opponents, in order to know what to expect from them, we need to be knowledgeable enough of Satan to know what to expect from him. We also need to know enough about how he works to recognize his work when we see it. With that in mind, take a look at some of Satan's most often-used marriage-destroying tactics.

- He is the father of lies. He plants untruths in your mind and on your lips. Once planted, they grow into more lies, deceptions, hurt feelings, angry outbursts, resentment, and separation of heart and mind.
- He is the accuser. Satan loves to speak accusations through anyone who lets him. He will use both of you to spew accusations such as, "You don't love me", "You don't appreciate me", "You don't respect me", "You don't ever want to do what I want to do", "You don't believe in me", "You aren't supportive", "You are such a momma's boy", "You will never be able to….", "You don't even try to look nice anymore", "You don't think I'm sexy anymore", "You don't realize how hard I work for what little money we have", "Do you even think about how much something costs before you buy it"…. I don't have to tell you what happens when accusations such as these start flying between the two of you.
- He is the adversary. Satan thrives on turmoil and conflict, so he does whatever he needs to do to pick a fight. He is especially thrilled when he is able to pick a fight between the two of you. He doesn't care what it's about. He knows that arguments easily lead to things being said that can't be unsaid or unheard; making it difficult to forgive and move forward in love.
- He is the powerful force in the realm of evil. Satan is responsible for the causes and effects of abuse, addiction, greed,

deception, sexual impurity, and every other kind of sin and evil. He tirelessly tries to force himself and these things into your life.

Satan is also known as the enemy, tempter, and thief. He has earned each of these titles and he wears them proudly. But he is proudest of all when he tears and shreds the union of a husband and wife who previously pledged to live as one for their whole life.

Prayer

Heavenly Father, be our buffer, our protector, and our weapon of defense against Satan. Give us the wisdom, insight, and strength to protect our marriage from the evil one. In the name of Jesus, amen.

TASK 1 NOW THAT YOU'VE BEEN REMINDED OF JUST HOW EVIL AND DETERMINED SATAN IS, TAKE ACTION. DON'T JUST READ THESE DESCRIPTIONS AND FACTS ABOUT SATAN AND MOVE ON. READ THEM AND THEN TAKE THE TIME TO TALK WITH ONE ANOTHER AND PUT TOGETHER A PLAN OF ATTACK TO MAKE SURE THAT WHEN MR. SATAN COMES KNOCKING, YOU SEND HIM PACKING.

___

Week Seventeen: When Mr. Satan Knocks

TASK 2

SPEAK TO SATAN EVERY SINGLE DAY, SAYING THIS ONE THING: "SATAN, YOU ARE NOT WELCOME IN OUR HOME. IN OUR MARRIAGE. IN OUR LIVES. WE DO NOT WANT YOU HERE. WE WILL NOT ALLOW YOU TO INFLUENCE US."

Week Eighteen: The Etiquette of Thankfulness

I give thanks to my God always for you because of the grace of God that was given you in Christ Jesus. ~ 1st Corinthians 1:4

Hannah was undoubtedly thankful for Elkanah's understanding and willingness to stand by Hannah's promise to give their son back to God. (1st Samuel 1) Both Jacob and Rachel were victims of magnanimous deceit, but don't you know they were both very thankful for each other? Jacob was thankful Rachel's love was strong enough to marry him and share him with her sister, and it isn't hard to understand why Rachel would be overwhelmed with thanks that Jacob's love for her was such that he was willing to work another seven years for her father—the one who had deceived them both. (Genesis 29) Jacob was no stranger to deceit, though, because he himself had schemed with his mother to deceive his father. The lies Rebekah concocted against her husband, Isaac, were horrendous! I honestly don't know how a marriage could survive something like that. But it did, and not only that, we read in Genesis 26, that they were laughing together and that they were in agreement that Esau made poor choices when it came to the women he married. Given the extreme amount of grace and forgiveness Rebekah had been shown by her husband, don't you think thankfulness was something she felt every day? Mary's attitude of thankfulness toward Joseph for believing her, believing the angel who told him Mary was a virgin, and for taking the journey with her to raise the Son of God…need I say more? Peter's wife was obviously a loving and generous woman and wife. Think about it—she welcomed Jesus and the disciples into her home knowing her husband would be traveling with the Savior instead of coming home to her every night. Peter was surely thankful for his understanding wife. Boaz and Ruth, Aquilla and Pricilla, Esther and Xerxes, Noah and Mrs. Noah, along with numerous other couples in the Bible all have their own lesson in thankfulness to share with us. Hopefully, they are lessons married couples like yourselves will take to heart… beginning now. Now that you've been reminded of the blessings of a good marriage, don't you think it would be wise to count the blessings in your marriage? Of course it is! So, that's what you are going to do…together. Be specific in your answers; recalling events and circumstances and revealing what turns your head and causes your heart to do that little flip-flop thing.

Please take this week's devotional time seriously. Your marriage will thank you for putting sincere thought and effort into it.

Prayer

Dear God, thank you for putting us together. I love my husband/wife and I am thankful for the life you are leading us to live. Bless our love. Bless our marriage. Bless our home. In Jesus' name, amen.

TASK 1
GET COMFY, PUT AWAY ANY AND ALL DISTRACTIONS (THAT INCLUDES PUTTING THE KIDS TO BED), AND FINISH THE FOLLOWING STATEMENTS

I am thankful for what I consider to be your top-three qualities:
___
___

I am thankful you are so willing to
___
___

I am thankful you take the time to
___
___

I am thankful for the time you
___
___

I am thankful you never
___
___

I am thankful you always
___
___

I am thankful you don't mind that I
___
___

I am thankful you support me in
___

Week Eighteen: The Etiquette of Thankfulness

I am thankful we made it through

I am thankful I can always count on you to

I am thankful you don't

I am thankful you want to

I am thankful that because I have you, I will never

I am thankful we have never

TASK 2

GO SHOPPING FOR A THANK-YOU GIFT FOR YOUR SPOUSE. DON'T SPEND MORE THAN $10—JUST A LITTLE SOMETHING FUN TO BRIGHTEN THEIR DAY AND LET THEM KNOW HOW MUCH THEY MEAN TO YOU.

Week Nineteen: It's All About That 'Tude

And whatever you do, in word or deed, do everything in the name of the Lord Jesus, giving thanks to God the Father through him.
~Colossians 3:17

Joe and Lucy are childhood sweethearts who have been married for nearly forty years. They've raised four amazing children and have weathered several storms that have erupted from time to time in their marriage. They've faced each of these storms with a strong faith in God and a commitment to make love the winner every time. This most recent storm, however, has the potential to overpower their relationship…if Joe doesn't have a change of attitude. Soon.

The problem is with one of their adult children. Joe had the daughter—we'll call her "Tessa".
When "Tessa" told her parents that she and her husband were separating and filing for divorce, the reasons she gave for the breakup of her marriage were not true. Rather than taking ownership of the part she played in the breakup of her marriage, she told her parents a story that painted her now ex-husband in a horrible, almost psychotic light.
When Joe and Lucy discovered their daughter had lied, their hurt, anger, and yes, even a bit of resentment toward "Tessa"

because of her lies, led to tension and verbal sparring. While Lucy has an attitude of "forgive because God has forgiven you", Joe and "Tessa" refuse to budge. Until an apology is offered by her dad, "Tessa" says a relationship is not possible. Joe says the same about "Tessa", yet neither of them believes they should have to apologize. So…

Both Joe and "Tessa's" attitude is causing serious problems. Not just for the two of them, but for the entire family. Lucy's heart is broken because of the fractures in her family—especially, she says, "…because it would all be made right if Joe and "Tessa's" attitudes were right—as in right in line with God's attitude about forgiveness."

Lucy is also disappointed in her husband. She sees his attitude as a declaration that his pride and need to be right are more important to him than she is. Than their family is. Thank God is.

What is your attitude when it comes to your marriage? No, the better question is this: Is your attitude about your marriage the same as God's?

This week's verse doesn't pick and choose what you do God's way vs. what you do your way. This week's verse tells us that everything…EVERYTHING we do and say should be done in the name of Jesus, i.e. the way Jesus would do it and using the words Jesus would use.

Unfortunately, having a Jesus attitude doesn't come as naturally to us as it should; seeing as how we are made in the image of God. But that's the consequences of sin, so we need to be extra-vigilant; always keeping our attitudes in check out of love for God and each other, and for the health and happiness of our marriage

Week Nineteen: It's All About That 'Tude

TASK 1: IN WHAT AREAS OF YOUR MARRIAGE DO YOU NEED AN ATTITUDE ADJUSTMENT?

_____
_____
_____
_____
_____
_____
_____
_____
_____
_____
_____
_____
_____
_____
_____
_____
_____
_____
_____
_____

Souls in Harmony

TASK 2: WHO OR WHAT PUSHES YOUR ATTITUDE BUTTONS? DO YOU REALIZE THESE PEOPLE OR THINGS AREN'T RESPONSIBLE FOR YOUR ATTITUDE—THAT YOU ARE COMPLETELY RESPONSIBLE FOR YOUR ACTIONS? WHAT ARE YOU GOING TO DO TO CHANGE HOW YOU LET THESE PEOPLE AND THINGS AFFECT YOU?

_____
_____
_____
_____
_____
_____
_____
_____
_____
_____
_____
_____
_____
_____
_____
_____
_____

TASK 3: WHAT CHANGES WOULD YOU LIKE TO ASK YOUR SPOUSE TO MAKE IN ORDER TO HELP YOU HAVE A BETTER ATTITUDE ABOUT THINGS?

_____
_____
_____
_____
_____
_____
_____
_____
_____
_____
_____
_____
_____
_____
_____
_____
_____
_____
_____
_____
_____
_____

Souls in Harmony

TASK 4: TAKE A FEW MINUTES TO WRITE THIS WEEK'S VERSE ON A FEW POST-IT NOTES. PLACE THEM AROUND THE HOUSE AND IN YOUR CAR TO REMIND YOU OF WHAT YOUR ATTITUDE SHOULD BE.

_____
_____
_____
_____
_____
_____
_____
_____
_____
_____
_____
_____
_____
_____
_____
_____
_____
_____
_____

Week Nineteen: It's All About That 'Tude

Week Twenty: Priorities... Priorities...Priorities

For where your treasure is, there will your heart be also. ~Luke 12:34

When Warren retired after thirty years as a law enforcement officer, he and his wife, Jody made another major life change. They turned the family farm over to their son and moved a hundred miles away to be closer to Warren's aging parents. Talk about turning your life upside down!

The first several months were rough. Warren didn't adjust to having so much time at home with very little to do. Jody, who'd always stayed home, had to adjust to a new house and community, and to not having her circle of friends and her kids and grandkids around. Neither one of them expected it to be as difficult as it was, and as a result, they found themselves arguing and taking their frustrations out on each other.

Accusations and arguments were the norm, and the air was thick with hurt feelings and resentment. Before either one of them realized it, Warren and Jody's marriage was in serious trouble. When Jody realized how serious things were, she insisted they sit down and talk things out—not argue.

By taking the time to really listen to each other, it became obvious that problem wasn't about Warren feeling left out when Jody went grocery shopping without him or Jody feeling guilty about going to lunch with a friend because she needed a break from Warren. The problem was priorities. Warren and Jody had to learn to adjust their priorities to include getting reacquainted in new surroundings and this new season of their life. And at the top of that list of priorities was open and honest communication and an added measure of grace as they established new routines that worked for both of them.

When God created the institution of marriage, he didn't put husbands and wives together so they could treat each other as last resort. But he doesn't expect us to give up our individuality, either. God doesn't expect us to be demanding, controlling, and manipulative. No way! God intends for husbands and wives to be companions, confidants, partners, and lovers.

God knows that when we make our marriage a priority second only to our relationship with God, good things happen. Good things, as in a marriage you can count on to be enjoyable, satisfying, and filled with love.

Prayer

LORD, take over my heart and mind. Fill me with the desire to put you first in all things and my marriage second. Help me be conscious of what my marriage needs and to put those needs at the top of my daily to-do list. In Jesus' name, amen.

TASK 1

WRITE DOWN WHAT YOU CONSIDER TO BE YOUR TOP FIVE PRIORITIES.

TASK 2 STARTING WITH 'GETTING OUT OF BED', LIST EVERY SINGLE THING YOU DO IN A 24-HOUR PERIOD. EVERYTHING. ABSOLUTELY EVERYTHING.

Week Twenty: Priorities…Priorities…Priorities

TASK 3
TAKE A LOOK AT BOTH LISTS. HOW WELL DOES YOUR DAILY ROUTINE MATCH UP TO AND REFLECT THE THINGS YOU LISTED AS YOUR PRIORITIES?

_____
_____
_____
_____
_____
_____
_____
_____
_____
_____
_____
_____
_____
_____
_____
_____
_____
_____
_____

TASK 4 ASK YOUR SPOUSE WHAT THEY BELIEVE YOU SHOULD DO TO MAKE YOUR MARRIAGE A HIGHER PRIORITY THAN IT IS RIGHT NOW. DISCUSS HOW THE TWO OF YOU CAN WORK TO MAKE THE REQUESTED ADJUSTMENTS.

Week Twenty: Priorities…Priorities…Priorities

Week Twenty-one: Accountability Factor

Brothers, if anyone is caught in any transgression, you who are spiritual should restore him in a spirit of gentleness. Keep watch on yourself, lest you too be tempted. ~Galatians 6:1

Over the course of the past several weeks, you have been reminded on several occasions of the importance of safeguarding your marriage against outside interference. You know, things like working way more than you should, choosing hobbies and friends over wife and family, and hiding out at home under the cover of social media, television, or video games. You've also been reminded on several occasions not to make your marital disputes the topic of discussion among your friends, mother, siblings, coworkers, or you kids. Especially your kids!! These reminders have always been accompanied by wise and practical reasons as to why you need to keep a hedge of privacy around your marriage; all of which are firmly rooted in God's teaching. But there are a few exceptions, and that is what we're going to focus on this week.

If you were to lump this elite group of exceptions together and give them a name, that name would be "Accountability". Accountability is defined as holding someone responsible for their actions. And let's be honest—we all need two or three someone's in our life we can count on to do that. It's easy to agree that we all need to be held accountable, but as long as we're being honest, we also need to admit actually putting yourself out there for people to 'grade' is another thing altogether. But that's not how it works.

Accountability is what I just said—putting yourself in the position to be called to task (held responsible) for your actions. Your words. Your attitude.

Take a minute to re-read that last paragraph a few times. Once you have it fixed firmly in your mind, read the following list of accountability factors and then do them—all of them that are applicable, that is.

- Choose two or three accountability partners. Aside from the obvious need to be able to trust these people with your heart and your deepest thoughts and questions, you also need to make sure your accountability partners meet the following criteria. Accountability partners are ALWAYS people who are the same sex as you are (guys choose guys, gals choose gals). No explanation as to why this is so, should be necessary. Accountability partners should always be Christians, to ensure the advice and admonishment you receive is always scriptural and God-honoring. It's usually best to choose accountability partners that are not family—at least not immediate family. This rule isn't set in stone, but choosing trusted friends usually keeps things in a more balanced perspective.
- Meet or talk regularly with your accountability partners. This isn't just about telling each other what you are doing wrong. This is about encouraging and praying for one another so that the 'wrongs' are the exceptions to the rule in your marriage relationship.
- When sharing with your accountability partners, only talk in terms of YOU/ME/I or US/WE…not him/her or he/she. This is about YOU being responsible in your marriage—not what your spouse is or isn't doing.

Week Twenty-one: Accountability Factor

- Pray for a pliable and supple heart and mind that isn't afraid to be restored in humility and grace.
- Be honest. You can't expect your accountability partners to hold you accountable if they don't know the truth.
- Okay, now that you know who and what an accountability partner is, let's talk about what things they need to hold you accountable for…
- Your relationships outside of marriage. Co-workers, friends, people at the gym, other soccer parents, your boss, and social media contacts should all be transparent and God-honoring.
- The way you talk, treat, and act around your spouse. Kindness matters. Are you willingly making yourself sexually available? Are you respecting your spouse?
- Your social media content, web browsing, television shows and movies, time spent away from your family, financial transparency with your spouse, modesty/dress, language, the places you go with friends, alcohol consumption, a spirit of nagging and/or complaining.
- Flirting (set clear boundaries as to what flirting is).
- The way you talk and interact with your spouse's family. Respect is key.
- Your obedience to God's Word; specifically loving your wife as Christ loves the Church and submission. Are you praying together? Serving and worshipping together?

This is quite a list, but these things are what make or break a marriage. As individuals, sometimes we fall into a routine of selfishness and neglecting our spouse without realizing what is taking place. Until it's too late. By aligning ourselves with Godly accountability partners, though, who will hold us (not our spouse) in check, we can make our marriages stronger as well as our relationships within God's family of brothers and sisters. And that, my friends, is a beautiful thing.

Prayer

God, send me accountability partners I can trust and depend on to keep me focused on what your desire for me as a spouse is. God, work through both of us as husband and wife to honor you with a marriage that is fulfilling and overflowing with the blessings that come from love. In Jesus' name, amen.

TASK 1

THIS WEEK'S HOMEWORK IS TO START OR BEEF UP THE ACCOUNTABILITY FACTOR IN YOUR MARRIAGE.

_____
_____
_____
_____
_____
_____
_____
_____
_____
_____
_____
_____
_____
_____
_____
_____
_____
_____
_____
_____
_____
_____

Week Twenty-two: I Did and I Still Do

Has not the one God made you? You belong to him in body and spirit. And what does the one God seek? Godly offspring. So be on your guard, and do not be unfaithful to the wife of your youth. ~Malachi 2:15

❝A wedding is saying "I do" when you're young and vibrant, and beautiful; full of hopes and dreams for the future and the energy to go after them. A marriage, on the other hand, is what happens when five…ten…twenty-five…forty…even sixty years later, youthful beauty is replaced by wrinkles and wisdom lines, when tiredness and fatigue are more the norm than vibrant, and when necessity, reality, and memories attach themselves to your hopes and dreams." ~Darla Noble

Weddings are wonderful, fun, and despite all the planning and preparation, weddings are also easy. Marriage done right is fulfilling, satisfying, trying, and full of compromise. It is also anything but easy. A wedding is a celebration of young love. Marriage is the experience of loving through the ages.

Life has a way of 'helping' us taking our marriage for granted, so from time to time, the truly wise and committed husbands and wives make an intentional effort to remind themselves just how sacred their marriage is. One of the best ways to do this to renew your vows from time to time.

Renewing your vows doesn't have to include a wedding-type setting. It can be done anywhere you choose. It can be just the two of you, or with family and friends. It's up to you. This week's homework is to do just that—to choose a place and time to renew your vows. To help you prepare your heart and mind for this special time, spend a few minutes answering the following questions and sharing your answers with one another.

NOTE: I have included the traditional wedding vows below, but feel free to write your own.

I (name) take you (name) to be my lawfully wedded husband/wife; To have and to hold from this day forward, for better or worse, richer or poorer, in sickness and in health, to love and to cherish; from this day forward until death do us part.

Prayer

God, thank you for my marriage. Help me always to hold the vows I took close to my heart and to honor them all the days of my life. In Jesus' name, amen.

TASK 1 HUSBANDS, TAKE A FEW MINUTES TO QUIETLY REFLECT ON WHY YOU DECIDED TO PROPOSE TO YOUR WIFE. WHAT WAS IT ABOUT HER THAT LED YOU TO KNOW THAT SHE WAS 'THE ONE'?

_____
_____
_____
_____
_____
_____
_____
_____
_____
_____
_____
_____
_____
_____
_____
_____

Week Twenty-two: I Did and I Still Do

TASK 2 WIVES, TAKE A FEW MINUTES TO QUIETLY REFLECT ON WHY YOU SAID YES. HOW DID YOU KNOW HE WAS 'THE ONE'?

_____
_____
_____
_____
_____
_____
_____
_____
_____
_____
_____
_____
_____
_____
_____
_____
_____
_____
_____
_____

Souls in Harmony

TASK 3
SPEND A FEW MINUTES TOGETHER, REFLECTING BACK TO YOUR WEDDING DAY—WHAT MADE IT SPECIAL? WHAT ARE YOUR MOST VIVID MEMORIES OF THE DAY AND WHY?

_____
_____
_____
_____
_____
_____
_____
_____
_____
_____
_____
_____
_____
_____
_____
_____
_____
_____
_____
_____

TASK 4

GET OUT THE WEDDING PICTURES AND LOOK AT THEM WITH YOUR CHILDREN. TELL THEM HOW YOU MET, SOME FUN DETAILS ABOUT YOUR DATING RELATIONSHIP, AND SOME DETAILS OF YOUR WEDDING.

_____
_____
_____
_____
_____
_____
_____
_____
_____
_____
_____
_____
_____
_____
_____
_____
_____
_____
_____

Souls in Harmony

Week Twenty-three: Listen to Your Body

At the end of ten days it was seen that they were better in appearance and fatter in flesh than all the youths who ate the king's food. ~Daniel 1:15

Laura loves being a wife and mom and gladly quit her job at a local bank to be a stay at home mom when their son, who is now four, was born. Two years later, she gave birth to twin boys, who are now chasing around after their older brother and discovering previously inconceivable things to do with blocks, Legos, playdough, and crayons.

With three very active little boys to look after all day long, plus laundry, cooking, and cleaning, Laura is constantly on the move. Her husband, Sam, is more than happy to share both parenting and household responsibilities when he gets home from his job as an elementary school teacher. He even puts off lesson plans and grading papers until after the boys are in bed and he and Laura have had some time alone to talk, relax, and to keep the romance and intimacy in their marriage strong.

Lately, however, Sam has felt Laura pulling away and making excuses for not having sex. Sam's hurt feelings started turning to suspicions. Was Laura being unfaithful? Had he said or done something to cause her to turn away from him? After a few weeks, Sam finally got up the courage to ask Laura straight up what the problem was.

When he asked if there was someone else, she started laughing and crying at the same time. "Someone else? When would I have time for someone else? And who would want me? I don't even like looking at my body, so why should you? Or anyone else?"

Sam took Laura in his arms and sat silently while she tearfully confessed how unhappy she was with her post-baby body, how guilty she felt for having those thoughts, and how desperately she wanted to feel good about herself again. By the time the conversation ended, Laura and Sam had worked out a plan for Sam to take the boys out of the house for a few hours on Sunday afternoons so Laura could meal prep. This would allow her to cook healthier meals for her and her family (which she loves to do). Sam also surprised Laura with a treadmill and a pair of bikes with pull-behind carts for the boys, so they can both get the exercise they want and need.

Six months later, Laura said to Sam, "When I got out of the shower this morning, I looked at myself in the mirror and for the first time in a long time, I was content. My body is never going to look like it did before the boys were born, but I know now that's okay, because my life is never going to be like it was before the boys were born and I wouldn't want it to be. God used me to form three amazing little people, and that should change me—physically, emotionally, and spiritually."

Later the following week at Bible study, Laura shared her testimony with the other women. In the discussion that followed, the women agreed that when we take care of our bodies by feeding them the way God created the human body to be fed, and when we exercise the muscles and joints to work the way God created them to, we will be happier and healthier from the inside out. And it's only when we are happy from the inside out that we can experience marriage (and every other kind of relationship) at its best.

Daniel was right. When we stick to eating only those foods God created for us to eat, and when get the proper amount of rest and exercise, we are physically, emotionally, and mentally better.

TASK 1
WHAT DO YOU LIKE ABOUT YOUR PHYSICAL APPEARANCE? YOUR PERSONALITY?

_____
_____
_____
_____
_____
_____
_____
_____
_____
_____
_____
_____
_____
_____
_____
_____
_____
_____
_____
_____
_____
_____

TASK 2

WHAT DON'T YOU LIKE ABOUT YOUR PHYSICAL APPEARANCE? YOUR PERSONALITY?

_____
_____
_____
_____
_____
_____
_____
_____
_____
_____
_____
_____
_____
_____
_____
_____
_____
_____
_____

Week Twenty-three: Listen to Your Body

TASK 3
SHARE YOUR LIST WITH YOUR SPOUSE AND DISCUSS HOW YOU MIGHT OVERCOME THE NEGATIVITY YOU FEEL.

_____
_____
_____
_____
_____
_____
_____
_____
_____
_____
_____
_____
_____
_____
_____
_____
_____
_____
_____
_____
_____
_____

TASK 4 CLEAN OUT YOUR PANTRY AND REFRIGERATOR; RIDDING IT OF UNHEALTHY JUNK FOOD AND PROCESSED FOODS. REPLACE THOSE THINGS WITH HEALTHY, FRESH FOODS.

_____
_____
_____
_____
_____
_____
_____
_____
_____
_____
_____
_____
_____
_____
_____
_____
_____

Week Twenty-three: Listen to Your Body

TASK 5

SET ASIDE TIME EACH DAY TO TAKE A WALK, JOG, OR RIDE A BIKE. START WITH 20 MINUTES A DAY AND WORK UP TO AN HOUR.

_____
_____
_____
_____
_____
_____
_____
_____
_____
_____
_____
_____
_____
_____
_____
_____
_____
_____
_____
_____

Week Twenty-four: Fingernails on the Chalkboard

Good sense makes one slow to anger, and it is his glory to overlook an offense. ~Proverbs 19:11

Mark complains Cindy never puts his tools back in the toolbox the right way and Cindy view's Mark not putting his dirty dishes in the dishwasher as a show of disrespect for her.

Larry's biggest pet peeve is a dirty car. Out of respect for her husband, Megan is careful to keep her car clean, but isn't nearly as concerned about it as Larry thinks she should be. Megan, on the other hand, wants to take all the crumbs Larry leaves on the breakfast table and put them in the floorboard of his car (just kidding).

Gracie is one of the most organized people you'll ever meet, which is one of the things her husband, Philip, loves best about her. He is the first to say his landscaping business wouldn't be the success that it is, if not for her organizational skills. Gracie appreciates her husband's trust and admiration, but what she really wants is his cooperation. He can't even remember to give her receipts for business purchases not billed directly to the business. "If he really appreciated my contributions to the business," Gracie says, "he wouldn't make it so difficult for me to keep things in order."

Those are just a few examples of some everyday annoyances couples deal with in their marriages. Little annoyances or pet peeves are bound to show themselves from time to time because we are all fallible and imperfect. No matter how much husbands and wives love one another, they are a union of one, they are still unique individuals with different personalities and different ways of thinking and doing things.

This week's verse is a great reminder that because we are different, our spouses will annoy us from time to time (or even day to day) like 'fingernails on the chalkboard'. But it's also a reminder that we will annoy them, too. Even taking that into consideration, we must remember that being different isn't wrong or bad. It's just …different. But when those differences come between a husband and wife, that's what makes them bad.

What about you? How well do you and your spouse handle the little differences that drive you up the wall? Do you see them through critical eyes or through eyes of grace? Are you disrespectful and unkind, or do you extend to them the grace you want extended to you? Do you expect your spouse to 'deal with it', or do you make an effort to do those things in such a way that is less troubling to them? Are you slow to anger for the good of your marriage and for the glory of God?

Prayer

God, I know neither of us is perfect, but help me take an honest look at myself and admit my faults. Give me the patience and wisdom to change so that I can eliminate a source of stress from my marriage. In Jesus' name, amen.

Souls in Harmony

TASK 1 IT'S BEEN PROVEN THAT WHEN YOU CHOOSE TO FOCUS ON THE POSITIVE INSTEAD OF THE NEGATIVE, THE NEGATIVE SEEMS LESS NEGATIVE. SO THAT'S WHAT YOU'RE GOING TO DO. MAKE A LIST OF ALL THE THINGS YOU LOVE ABOUT YOUR SPOUSE.

_____
_____
_____
_____
_____
_____
_____
_____
_____
_____
_____
_____
_____
_____
_____
_____
_____

Week Twenty-four: Fingernails on the Chalkboard

TASK 2
READ THE LIST TO YOUR SPOUSE AND THANK THEM FOR POSSESSING THESE TRAITS.

TASK 3 EVERY DAY FOR THE NEXT WEEK (AT LEAST), GIVE GOD THANKS FOR EVERYTHING ON THE LIST; NAMING THEM INDIVIDUALLY.

_____
_____
_____
_____
_____
_____
_____
_____
_____
_____
_____
_____
_____
_____
_____
_____
_____

Week Twenty-four: Fingernails on the Chalkboard

TASK 4 Think about the things you know you do that irritates your spouse. Don't talk about them but decide in your heart and mind to stop doing these things. Do you notice any changes in your relationship?

_____
_____
_____
_____
_____
_____
_____
_____
_____
_____
_____
_____
_____
_____
_____
_____
_____
_____
_____
_____

Week Twenty-five: Because...

In the movie "Sweet Home Alabama", the opening scene shows a tween-age boy and girl on the sandy bank of the river. It's storming and much to the dismay of every mom on the planet, these kids are sticking metal poles in the sand... while it is lightening. On top of all that drama, comes the moment when the two little sweethearts share a little kiss. At this point Melanie tells Jake she's going to marry him someday. He responds by asking, "What do you want to marry me for, anyhow?", to which she replies, "So I can kiss you anytime I want."

That's one good reason, I guess, because God most definitely wants us to be physically and sexually attracted to your mate. But we also know that being a good kisser is NOT the only reason for choosing and loving your spouse and that the reasons you have to be thankful for your husband or wife are likely to be different from someone else's...specifically-speaking, anyway.
That's what you are going to do this week—focus on all the reasons you have to brag on your spouse. But before you get started (because once you start you won't want to stop), take a few minutes to read the following passages of scripture—all of which reveal deep levels of admiration, devotion, respect, and love for one another.

When a man takes a new wife, he shall not go out with the army nor be charged with any duty; he shall be free at home one year and shall give happiness to his wife whom he has taken. ~Deuteronomy 24:5

Week Twenty-five: Because...

The phrase you need to pay special attention to in this verse is, "…and shall give happiness to his wife….".

Among the misconceptions many people have about the Bible, is the misconception that women were nothing more than property. While there were undoubtedly marriages in which the wife was not cherished and respected as she should have been, isn't the same things true even today? The truth of the matter is that most of the women we read about in the Bible were dearly loved, highly respected, and cherished and cared for by their husbands—just like God wants them to be.

For a husband to be released from military responsibilities for an entire year, 'just' because he got married, is a pretty big deal. Don't you agree? It says quite a bit about their relationship, and if he takes these instructions to heart, his bride will have plenty of reasons to sing his praises and compliment his efforts.

> …*You have made my heart beat faster with a single glance of your eyes…How much better is your love than wine…. ~Ecclesiastes 4:9b-10*

The chemistry and desire between this man and his bride is palpable. The compliments he gives her are obviously sincere and heart-felt. Any woman who is on the receiving end of such admiration is going to be more than ready to be a devoted and loving wife, because sharing love back is one of the easiest and most pleasurable things to do.

Her worth is far above jewels. The heart of her husband trusts in her, and he will have no lack of gain…. She considers a field and buys it; from her earnings she plants a vineyard…. Strength and dignity are her clothing, and she smiles at the future. She opens her mouth in wisdom, and the teaching of kindness is on her tongue…. Her children rise up and bless her; her husband also, and he praises her, saying:

"Many daughters have done nobly, but you excel them all." ~From Proverbs 31

Priceless. Trustworthy. Strong, dignified, and hopeful. Wise. Kind. A loving and nurturing mother. Accomplished. Does this sound like a man who doesn't cherish the woman he's married to? Does this sound like a man who isn't setting an example for his children to honor their mother?
Dorothy Law Nolte wrote "Children Learn What They Live" in 1924. Wouldn't you agree, though, that children aren't the only ones this timeless poem applies to? Husbands and wives are just as 'guilty' of living up (or down) to what is expected of them.

Prayer

LORD, Thank you for giving me such a loving, Godly spouse. Help me to always honor my mate by letting them know just how much he/she means to me. Amen.

Week Twenty-five: Because…

TASK 1
MAKE A LIST OF AS MANY OF YOUR SPOUSE'S POSITIVE ATTRIBUTES THAT YOU CAN THINK OF.

_____

_____

_____

_____

_____

_____

_____

_____

_____

_____

_____

_____

_____

_____

_____

_____

_____

_____

_____

_____

TASK 2
MAKE A LIST OF THREE TO FIVE THINGS YOU HOPE YOUR SPOUSE HAS ON HIS/HER LIST OF YOUR POSITIVE ATTRIBUTES.

Week Twenty-five: Because…

TASK 3 CHOOSE AT LEAST THREE OF THE FOLLOWING METHODS FOR COMPLIMENTING AND PRAISING YOUR SPOUSE FOR BEING THEIR WONDERFUL, AMAZING SELF.

- Write a love letter

_____

_____

- Recreate your first date or another special date and tell him/her when and why you realized they were the one you wanted to spend your life with.

_____

_____

- Surprise your spouse with a special little gift (nothing too expensive) and attach a note saying, "Just because you are so.... (list some of their wonderful qualities).

_____

_____

- Write a poem or song for your husband/wife.

_____

_____

- Give your spouse the gift of time to do something they enjoy (a manicure, a round of golf, tickets to the game with a buddy, a gift card to her favorite store, a day alone at home to do anything or nothing), along with a note telling them why you want to give them this time off.

_____

_____

NOTES

_____
_____
_____
_____
_____
_____
_____
_____
_____
_____
_____
_____
_____
_____
_____
_____
_____
_____
_____

Week Twenty-five: Because…

Week Twenty-six: In Times Like These

For I am convinced that neither death nor life, neither angels nor demons, neither the present nor the future, nor any powers, neither height nor depth, nor anything else in all creation, will be able to separate us from the love of God that is in Christ Jesus our Lord.
~Romans 8:38-39

Keith and Leann were both raised in solid Christian homes, so it was no surprise to anyone that they gave God first place in their marriage and in their home. Keith and Leann's faith was definitely put to the test four years later when Leann went for what she thought was a routine prenatal visit in the fourth month of her second pregnancy. When the doctor came into the examining room, she told Leann that the bloodwork they'd taken the previous month showed some slight abnormalities, so she thought it would be a good idea to get some x-rays. Less than an hour later, Leann sat in a different examination room waiting for the doctor to discuss the results. She was a little nervous thinking about what abnormalities might be, but when the nurse came in to see if Leann needed or wanted anything, Leann couldn't help but notice how nervous and attentive the nurse was. "Is everything okay?" Leann asked. "The doctor will be in in a couple of minutes and she'll go over everything," the nurse answered softly, with a weak smile. Then almost as an afterthought, she asked, "Are you here by yourself, or is someone in the waiting room?"

Now Leann was really nervous. That's not a question they would normally ask.

A short time later Leann knew full-well why the nurse had asked her such a strange question.

"The baby's brain stem is only partially developed. His development will continue at a drastically slowed rate—where it continues at all…I will do my best to answer the questions I know you have, but I highly recommend you terminate the pregnancy as soon as possible to limit the emotional and physical trauma….Leann, are you by yourself, or is there someone in the waiting room who can…."

No, she had come alone, but yes, she would like to call Keith. Yes, of course I have questions, but no, I will not terminate the pregnancy, so there is no use talking about it. All of these thoughts, plus oodles of questions, were gushing through Leann's mind at once.

Fast-forward four months to a hot sunny, September day. The sun's warmth wasn't enough, however, to take away the numbing cold that grips you when you know this is the day you will bury your child in the ground.

Keith and Leann's baby had taken both his first and last breaths three days earlier. Seven short hours is all they were given to love on their son, but that was six more hours than they had been told to expect, so they were thankful and had cherished each and every second.

Yes, thankful. They were thankful for the extra time mercifully given by the God who would now sustain them through their grief. Thankful for the smell of his fuzzy head of hair, the feel of his soft skin, and the miracle of a few brief moments where his eyes opened, and he looked intently at both the mom and dad who loved him so deeply.

Week Twenty-six: In Times Like These

Thankful for the faith and convictions that guided them to this moment instead of taking what had been described as the 'easy' and 'least painful' solution—terminating the pregnancy due to its irreparable

And now here they were standing at the front of the church thanking family and friends for sharing this difficult time with them. They asked for prayers in the coming days, weeks, and months ahead for comfort and healing. They asked that those gathered there would also see the joy and miracle of Isaiah's short life instead of what it might have been.

And then they sang.

Keith and Leann sang a song of praise to God that he is able to sustain us through anything—even death. They sang that even when we don't understand, when we don't want to do things God's way, and when we aren't able to speak a word, God is able to work through us and for us, as long as we remember that he is Holy God.

Wow! What a testimony, right? It's one of those things that leaves a lot of us feeling humble and grateful. It shines the light of perspective on whatever it is you are dealing with. It also reminds you that nothing will destroy your faith in God and your love for one another as long as you allow the Holy Spirit to stand guard over both. But there's also a chance that reading Keith and Leann's story causes you to feel ashamed and alone. They were able to power through their pain and suffering by holding on to their faith and each other, so why couldn't you? Regardless of which voice is yours, you need to remember these things:

- Tragedies, sickness, and death are not the only issues that can tear you away from God and each other. Anything you don't agree on or anything that causes disruption in your marriage can sever your relationship if you let it.
- Keith and Leann's faith and marriage weren't made

strong because of what happened. Their strong faith and marriage gave them what they needed to survive their son's death.

You cannot wait until 'times like these' to build a stronger marriage and grow your faith. The human heart and mind don't work like that. If those things aren't already in place for us to take shelter in, we fall back on our instincts to survive at all costs.

When faith and marriage relationships grow strongER in 'times like these', it's because the foundation was already solidly in place—a foundation that is cared for and nourished every single day.

Remember:

Let not steadfast love and faithfulness forsake you; bind them around your neck; write them on the tablet of your heart. So you will find favor and good success in the sight of God and man. ~Proverbs 3:3-4 (ESV)

TASK 1 — WHAT ARE YOU DOING TODAY, TOMORROW, AND EVERY DAY HEREAFTER TO SECURE THE FOUNDATION OF YOUR MARRIAGE?

_____
_____
_____
_____
_____
_____
_____
_____
_____
_____
_____
_____
_____
_____
_____
_____
_____
_____
_____
_____

TASK 2
WHAT ARE YOU DOING TO BECOME MORE KNOWLEDGEABLE OF AND IN TUNE WITH GOD?

_____
_____
_____
_____
_____
_____
_____
_____
_____
_____
_____
_____
_____
_____
_____
_____
_____
_____
_____
_____

Week Twenty-six: In Times Like These

TASK 3

WHAT PEOPLE, SITUATIONS, AND CIRCUMSTANCES HAVE CHALLENGED YOUR MARRIAGE AND YOUR FAITH? HOW DID YOU RESPOND? DO YOU BELIEVE YOUR BOTH YOUR FAITH AND YOUR MARRIAGE GREW STRONGER BECAUSE OF THESE THINGS? WHY OR WHY NOT?

_____
_____
_____
_____
_____
_____
_____
_____
_____
_____
_____
_____
_____
_____
_____
_____
_____
_____
_____
_____

TASK 4 — SET ASIDE SOME TIME THIS WEEK TO HAVE AN HONEST DISCUSSION WITH EACH OTHER ABOUT CURRENT OR POSSIBLY HARDSHIPS IN YOUR MARRIAGE.

Examples: aging parents, a rebellious child, financial hardships, chronic illness, relocating, tension between either of you and your adult children and/or extended family members. Discuss possible ways of dealing with these situations based on what the Bible has to say and your own thoughts and feelings. Work hard to come to an agreement on how these things will be handled…together.

_____
_____
_____
_____
_____
_____
_____
_____
_____
_____
_____
_____
_____
_____
_____
_____

TASK 5
MEMORIZE THIS WEEK'S VERSE(S): ROMANS 8:38-39. PRAY THESE WORDS WITH YOUR SPOUSE ON A REGULAR BASIS.

Week Twenty-seven: Road Work Ahead

With all humility and gentleness, with patience, bearing with one another in love, eager to maintain the unity of the Spirit in the bond of peace. ~Ephesians 4:2-3

Anyone who gets behind the wheel of a car knows about traffic. The constant stream of car and trucks moving…coasting…speeding down the streets and highways we drive on is mind-boggling. Where do they all come from? Where are they all going? Or, if you are like John, who is retired, and asks every time he goes to the market midday and sees the parking lot full of cars, "Doesn't anyone go to work?" We won't ever come face to face with most of the people we share the road with, will we? And passing someone on the interstate, or waiting in adjoining lanes at a stoplight is the only time you will ever encounter the majority of the people you share the road with, isn't it? Yet even these brief, one-time, meaningless encounters are still just that—encounters. What's more, they might not be as meaningless as you think. Every vehicle leaves its mark wherever it goes. What I mean, is that every set of tires makes an indention in the pavement. Of course it's not noticeable or measurable on its own, but when you add the indentions of a gazillion vehicles all together, you get ruts in the road. All those tires leaving their mark eventually presses the pavement down to show the 'world' they were there.

By now I know you are dying to know how tire treads and ruts in the road could possible have anything to do with being married. Or at the very least, you are bound to be a little curious, right? Okay—here it is…

Every time you take each other for granted, choose self over spouse, or assume that the fact that you're still there is proof enough of your love, you are wearing a rut in the road of your marriage, so to speak. And just in case you don't already know—that's not a good thing.

Yes, there are lots of things we settle in to over the years—things that make our marriages comfortable and predictable. Neither of these things (comfort and predictability) is a bad thing—not always, anyway. There's a lot of great things to be said about comfort and predictability in a marriage. What you need to be careful of, however, is that you don't confuse comfort and predictability with negligence and indifference.

Take a minute to let that last statement sink in.

Is it there? Good, now let's look at some things you can do to make sure this doesn't become the case in your marriage. Marriage, remember, is a union. But even the strongest bonds wear down over time, and if you don't put any effort into maintaining those bonds of unity. Without maintenance, they break down and eventually collapse. So, put on your work clothes, gather up your tools, and get ready to take your marriage for a sweet ride (pun intended).

Prayer

LORD, thank you for the one I am sharing my life with. Help me to always be conscious and eager to keep the bonds of my marriage strong and vital. In Jesus' name, amen.

Souls in Harmony

TASK 1 ASK YOURSELF THE FOLLOWING QUESTIONS.

- When did you give your wife flowers?

  _____
  _____
  _____

- When is the last time you complimented your spouse?

  _____
  _____
  _____

- How often do you say positive things about your spouse to your friends?

  _____
  _____
  _____

- How often do you tell your spouse, "I love you."?

  _____
  _____
  _____

- Are you tender and appropriately affectionate with your spouse in front of the kids?

  _____

_____

_____

- Do you prove your trust in each other by being transparent with your finances, your feelings, and in expressing your needs and wants?

_____

_____

_____

- When is the last time you cooked your husband's favorite dinner?

_____

_____

_____

- When is the last time you told your spouse they are beautiful/handsome, sexy, smart, a great parent, your best friend?

Based on your answers, what kind of road work do you need to do?

_____

_____

_____

TASK 2 IF YOU HAVE KIDS, PUT THEM TO BED EARLY, OR BETTER YET, SEND THEM TO GRANDMA'S FOR A SLEEPOVER, SO YOU CAN SPEND THE EVENING CUDDLING, DANCING, TALKING, AND WHATEVER ELSE YOU WANT TO DO... TOGETHER.

_____
_____
_____
_____
_____
_____
_____
_____
_____
_____
_____
_____
_____
_____
_____
_____

TASK 3 Think about the things you have done over the past few weeks that might have hurt your spouses' feelings. Did you say (or not say) something you shouldn't (or should) have? Did you fail to notice his/her efforts? Did you criticize instead of compliment? Did you complain instead of finding out why? Did you ignore a request to fix, find, or help? Did you fail to see he/she needed a helping hand and then be that extra set of hands? Go to your spouse, own your mistakes, and ask him or her to forgive you.

TASK 4 ASK YOUR SPOUSE THIS QUESTION: WHAT CAN I DO TODAY TO MAKE YOUR DAY EASIER AND BETTER? THEN DO IT.

Week Twenty-seven: Road Work Ahead

TASK 5

Every smart couple takes time once or twice a year to reassess the goals they have for their marriage, family, and for themselves. Now is that time for you. It doesn't have to be anything formal—no documents or contracts are necessary. Prayer, conversation, and a mindset of unity is all that's necessary.

Week Twenty-eight: It's Okay to Ask for Help

Your testimonies are my delight; they are my counselors. ~Psalm 119:24

We're more than half-way through this book of weekly devotionals, which means we're more than half-way through the year. Over the course of the last few months you've discovered (or rediscovered) the importance of making your marriage a priority second only to God. We've also talked about the importance of protecting your union from outside interferences that can lead to anything from indifference, to infidelity. Interferences such as these are why nearly half of all marriages end in divorce. Even Christian marriages. Yours doesn't have to be one of them. And one of the best ways to protect your marriage is to seek out positive influences (vs. interferences) for your relationship. Influences like… Ralph and Tessie. "Ralph and Tessie were like another set of parents to us. They loved us, loved our kids, and welcomed us into their lives in a way that was as natural as anything. They didn't talk about how to do marriage. They just did it and did it well. It was through watching them, listening to them, and being with them that we learned what things like 'in sickness and in health', compromise, selflessness, and agreeing to disagree look like when done out of a heart, soul, and mind of love." ~Cora

Ellen and David. "Ellen and David were childhood sweethearts and married when Ellen was fifteen and David was seventeen— just days before David, a Marine, was sent overseas. No, Ellen wasn't pregnant, and no, the year wasn't 1940-something. It was 2012. Seven years, two little girls, two overseas deployments, and three duty stations later, this Godly young family is an example to everyone they meet. Their humble and total commitment to God and to one another is an inspiration to the church families they become a part of no matter where they live, to their family and friends (young and old), and to countless military personnel and their families. Just watching them be 'them' is a powerful influence in the lives of others. Adam and Carissa. On the day of their ninth wedding anniversary, Carissa dropped their three year-old daughter off at a friends so that she and Adam could enjoy a few hours together before he had to be back on campus for a major event to welcome incoming freshmen to the Christian campus ministry he led. The couple chose to spend their time taking a leisurely ride on Adam's motorcycle. About an hour into the ride they headed down a quiet county road that had recently been repaved. Going only 10 or 15 mph, Adam unexpectedly hit a pile of loose gravel. In a matter of seconds, Adam went from being active and athletic, to a quadriplegic. Needless to say, it turned their lives upside down. But they held on—to God, to one another, and to their family and friends. Fifteen years later, they are still happily married, Adam still preaches and teaches (in a church), Carissa uses her talents for God in many ways, and the are very happily married. Has it been easy? No! But when asked, they don't hesitate to say that quitting was never an option for either of them. In sharing their story, these two have influenced dozens, if not hundreds of young couples preparing for marriage. Do you see how these influences are touching lives simply by being faithful? By being a living, breathing example of what scripture says about marriage? Their influence and mentorship aren't of academic or intellectual, even. It's spiritual and relational. That isn't to say you should never ask someone to share their story or ask for advice and Godly counsel. If you need it—ask for it. 2nd Corinthians 1:3-4 says, Praise be to the God and Father of our Lord Jesus Christ, the Father of compassion and the God of all comfort, who comforts us in all our troubles, so that we can comfort those in any trouble with the comfort we ourselves receive from God.

These two verses are really what mentoring is all about. It's riding out your problems, dealing with difficult situations, working through pain and grief, and taking life step by step, one day at a time holding tight to the Savior's hand so that you can grow in faith AND nurture the faith of others.
Do you have mentors and influences in your marriage? Are you setting an example for others?

Prayer

LORD, keep my marriage safe from interferences. Help me learn from the wisdom of others how to make our marriage one of faith in you and each other. In Jesus' name, amen.

TASK 1 — WHOSE MARRIAGES DO YOU ADMIRE AND WHY?

_____
_____
_____
_____
_____
_____
_____
_____
_____
_____
_____
_____
_____
_____
_____
_____
_____
_____
_____
_____

Souls in Harmony

TASK 2
WHEN YOU HAVE A PROBLEM IN YOUR MARRIAGE, WHO DO YOU GO TO?

_____
_____
_____
_____
_____
_____
_____
_____
_____
_____
_____
_____
_____
_____
_____
_____
_____
_____

Week Twenty-eight: It's Okay to Ask for Help

TASK 3
TAKE SOME TIME TO READ ABOUT SOME OF THE MORE INFAMOUS MARRIAGES IN THE BIBLE THIS WEEK. WHAT MADE THESE MARRIAGES STRONG OR PROBLEMATIC? WHAT LESSONS ARE THERE TO BE LEARNED FROM EACH OF THESE COUPLES?

- Abraham and Sarah

- Isaac and Rebekah

- Elkanah and Hannah

- Pricilla and Aquilla

- Queen Esther and King Xerxes

- Boaz and Naomi

- Samson and Delilah

Souls in Harmony

TASK 4 CHOOSE ONE OR TWO COUPLES WHOSE MARRIAGE YOU ADMIRE. INVITE THEM TO YOUR HOME OR TAKE DESSERT AND VISIT THEM IN THEIRS. ASK THEM TO SHARE WHAT THEY BELIEVE TO BE THE REASONS FOR THEIR MARTIAL SUCCESS AND HAPPINESS.

_____
_____
_____
_____
_____
_____
_____
_____
_____
_____
_____
_____
_____
_____
_____
_____
_____
_____

Week Twenty-eight: It's Okay to Ask for Help

Week Twenty-nine: When One + One + One Doesn't Equal One

But seek first the kingdom of God and his righteousness, and all these things will be added to you. ~Matthew 6:33

We mentioned last week the fact that nearly half of all marriages fail, and that these statistics were sadly no different among Christians than they are among non-Christians. Why is that? Why are marriages among believers crumbling as often and as tragically as other marriages?

The answer to that question is God. Or more precisely, the absence of God. Just because someone says they are a Christian doesn't mean they are. Just because someone shows up at church every Sunday, and maybe even participates in church activities doesn't make them a true Christian. Just because someone wears a t-shirt that says "All I need is mascara and Jesus" doesn't make them a wife completely sold out for Jesus and her marriage. Just because a guy plays on the church softball team every week doesn't mean he's really on God's team. Sound harsh? Maybe even a bit…dare I say it…judgmental?
It is neither. It is hard truth—not harsh truth. And as for

being judgmental, no. When a person's life doesn't reflect their declarations of faith and obedience, that's not judgment. That's accountability. You see, Christianity isn't something you do. It's something you are; something that becomes part of your person. Your heart, soul, and mind. That leaves us with the question of how to make for sure and for certain that God is at the center of your marriage, surrounding it like a warm, fuzzy blanket, AND as an impenetrable force.

The answers to that question are:

- Pray together. Pray for one another. Pray for your marriage. Pray for your family, for sound judgment, discernment, patience, perseverance, humility, selflessness, and faith.
- Know God's Word. Read it. Study it. Memorize key verses that speak to your heart.
- Serve God and others together.
- Serve one another.
- Worship together.
- Communicate. Don't assume, talk. And when you talk, say what you mean and mean what you say.
- Blanket your home in scripture. When you decorate your home with scripture and Godly encouragements, you will be reminded of God's truth consciously and subconsciously. That's a good thing.
- Use the wisdom and instruction of the Bible and the blessing of prayer when making decisions.
- Remove or place firm boundaries on any and all things from your home and your marriage that tempt you away from God: television shows, movies, books, video games, access to websites, social media, outside relationships, outside activities, and even your children.

This is NOT to say any of these things are bad or that you should never enjoy any of these things individually or as a couple. You simply need to remember that your marriage comes first. As

Week Twenty-nine: When One + One + One Doesn't Equal One

for your children, make sure you always present a united front when it comes to parenting and work out any differences in opinion you have about parenting in private. Remember—the way you fulfill your roles as husband and wife are the model your children will someday take into their marriage relationship. God blessed Rebekah with twins after years of barrenness. He also gave her a glimpse into the future lives of her children by telling her the older twin would serve the younger. Had Rebekah and Isaac been committed to keeping God in the center of their marriage, she wouldn't have taken matters into her own hands; resulting in the fracturing her family beyond repair.

Joseph and Mary, on the other hand, chose to follow God rather than their inclinations to run and hide, or refuse to do what God asked them to do. That's right—they had the choice to obey or not. Praise God they chose to obey in faith.

It's easy to see the differences in these two marriages. It should also be easy to decide which one you want your own marriage to look like.

Prayer

God, we want you to be the center and protector of our marriage. We welcome you to insert yourself in all areas of our marriage; guiding and teaching us to be obedient, trusting, and committed to you and to one another. Amen.

TASK 1 TAKE ANOTHER LOOK AT THE LIST OF WAYS TO PUT A GOD-HEDGE AROUND YOUR MARRIAGE. DECIDE TOGETHER HOW YOU WILL INCORPORATE EACH OF THESE INTO YOUR MARRIAGE. OR IF YOU ARE ALREADY DOING ANY/ALL OF THEM, HOW CAN YOU TAKE IT UP A NOTCH.

_____
_____
_____
_____
_____
_____
_____
_____
_____
_____
_____
_____
_____
_____
_____
_____

Week Twenty-nine: When One + One + One Doesn't Equal One

Week Thirty: Romance Rekindled

How beautiful and pleasant you are, O loved one, with all your delights! ~Song of Solomon 7:6

Matt and Callie appeared to be happily married to those on the outside looking in. But Callie's parents were troubled because the two were never affectionate with one another. No hugs, kisses, hand holding…nothing, really, to indicate there was any romance in their marriage. When Callie told her parents the two were separating and filing for divorce, they were sad and disappointed that the marriage was ending, but they weren't surprised, because intimacy and romance are essential to a healthy marriage. Even a Christian marriage. Especially a Christian marriage.

Let's just be honest here—the Bible isn't usually our first go-to when it comes to getting ideas on how to romance your husband or wife or talk about God and sex in the same sentence. Oh, I know—intellect and faith tell us God created us to be sexual beings and all that entails, aka intercourse and the pleasures it brings. But to talk about sex and God in the same sentence, or to think about God being interested in your sex life, well, that just doesn't seem appropriate or…right. But it is—both right and appropriate.

The Song of Solomon is a love story of a couple who are

engaged and then married. Its descriptive passages are strange to us, because in today's society, we would never even think about comparing a beautiful woman to a goat or any other animal, for that matter. But the message is clear—these two are on fire for each other. They aren't the only ones, though. Isaac and Rebekah, Jacob and Rachel, Pilate and Mrs. Pilate, David and Bathsheba, NS Hannah and Elkanah are just a few of the couples in the Bible whose tender love for one another is evident in reading about them. Despite the fact that the word romance doesn't appear in the Bible, there are several examples of what it is and isn't. The truth of the matter is that God is very much interested in your romantic life. God knows that the need for romantic and sexual fulfillment is strong, so he is very much in favor of couples keeping romance and sexual intimacy alive and well in their marriage. This in no way implies romance and sex are to be the foundations of a marriage, because they aren't. Romance and marriage are expressions and of a deeper love— the love describe in 1st Corinthians 13. The love that really is there for better or worse, sickness and health…. What about your marriage? What do you do to keep the romance alive in your marriage?

Prayer

God, thank you for romance and for sex. Help me to not feel embarrassed about being romantic with my spouse and don't let me fall into the habit of taking him/her for granted. Amen.

Week Thirty: Romance Rekindled

TASK 1

Use the following list of ideas to help you be more intentional in romancing your spouse. It doesn't matter whether you've been married 1, 10, 30, or even 60 years—romance is important in a marriage.

- Write your spouse a love note.
  _____
  _____

- Kiss each other good morning and good night.
  _____
  _____

- Hold hands while taking a walk, in church, and when you pray together.
  _____
  _____

- Have dinner by candlelight once in a while—even if it's frozen pizza or a can of soup.
  _____
  _____

- Play 'your song' once in a while when you settle into bed for the night and just hold each other.
  _____
  _____

- Check into a hotel for the night and pretend it's your honeymoon all over again.

- Surprise your spouse by doing some of their regular household chores for them.

- Call just to say, "I love you".

- Tell your kids how blessed you feel that God gave you their dad or mom to be your husband or wife.

- Men, be chivalrous.

- Ladies, the time to put on sexy lingerie for bed once in a while.

Week Thirty: Romance Rekindled

TASK 2
TALK TO ONE ANOTHER ABOUT YOUR ROMANTIC AND SEXUAL NEEDS AND DESIRES SO THAT YOU WILL KNOW WHAT EACH OF YOU NEEDS IN ORDER TO BE SATISFIED.T

_____
_____
_____
_____
_____
_____
_____
_____
_____
_____
_____
_____
_____
_____
_____
_____
_____
_____
_____
_____
_____
_____

Week Thirty-one: A Slow Leak

Repay no one evil for evil, but give thought to do what is honorable in the sight of all. If possible, so far as it depends on you, live peaceably with all. ~Romans 12:17-18

Leslie is annoyed that Tim leave crumbs all over the table after eating. Was it so hard to brush them into his hand and put them in the sink or the trash? And while we're on the subject of annoyances, is there a rule she isn't aware of that says the wife always has to be the one to fill the hot water pot so it will be ready for tea or coffee? In Leslie's defense, she has asked Tim to be more conscientious of these things, but since these things aren't important to him, his response has been to ignore his wife's requests.

Tim doesn't think those things are a big deal, but he sure gets bent out of shape when they are in Leslie's car and her phone rings through her Bluetooth. He didn't talk to her for three hours one day because she said she wasn't going to unlink the phone from the car when they were in there together.

If you were to ask Leslie and Tim if they are happy in their marriage, I have no doubt the answer would be yes. Or maybe, yes, but....

While none of Leslie and Tim's annoyances are what most people would consider marriage breakers, they most certainly could be. Husbands and wives don't wake up one morning and decide that's the day they are going to have an affair, that they are going to become an addict, or that they are so bored with their marriage that anything would be better than staying. Dysfunction in a marriage happens over time. It's like a slow leak in a beach ball. You notice the ball doesn't travel as far and sounds a little hollow when you hit it, but you just keep playing with it. Then one day the air is gone and it's flat. Letting those little annoyances build up; playing the 'game' of getting even or tit for tat instead of addressing them honestly and fairly, is a recipe for disaster. Annoyances turn to resentment. Resentment turns to anger. Anger turns to bitterness. Bitterness turns to rage that expresses itself in lies, criticism, deceit, infidelity, and ultimately, divorce. Getting on each other's nerves from time to time is inevitable. None of us is perfect and none of us will do everything the way we think they should. The operative word here is 'us'. Not just one person in a marriage is guilty of being annoying. Neither should just one person be 'guilty' of giving grace and doing what is honorable to keep peace.

Prayer

God, Pour your grace and mercy into me so that it overflows out of my heart and into my marriage. Help me see myself as a flawed, imperfect individual with a perfect Savior. In Jesus' name, amen.

TASK 1 WRITE DOWN THE THINGS YOUR SPOUSE DOES TO ANNOY YOU. NOW MAKE A LIST OF ALL REASONS YOU ARE THANKFUL FOR YOUR SPOUSE AND THE THINGS THEY DO THAT MAKE YOU SMILE. IF YOUR LIST OF ANNOYANCES IS LONGER, YOU HAVE WORK TO DO. YES, YOU. YOU NEED TO EXAMINE YOUR HEART AND LET GO OF THE HABIT OF BEING SO CRITICAL.

_____
_____
_____
_____
_____
_____
_____
_____
_____
_____
_____
_____
_____
_____
_____
_____
_____

Week Thirty-one: A Slow Leak

TASK 2

Stop and think about the things your spouse finds annoying in you. Try seeing things from their perspective and make whatever changes you can make with a joyful heart to make your spouse happy.

_____
_____
_____
_____
_____
_____
_____
_____
_____
_____
_____
_____
_____
_____
_____
_____
_____
_____
_____
_____

TASK 3 PRAY FOR YOUR MARRIAGE. PRAY FOR YOUR ATTITUDE.

Week Thirty-one: A Slow Leak

Week Thirty-two: Praying Your Way to Happiness

Continue steadfastly in prayer, being watchful in it with thanksgiving. ~Colossians 4:2

Beau and Kathrine were both raised in Christian homes and raised their four children to know and love the LORD, too. But Beau will admit that even though he's approaching middle age, he still struggles with giving God total control. Having spent 30 years in law enforcement, Beau is used to keeping his guard up and always being self-controlled and in control of his surroundings.

Katherine understands why her husband struggles in this area, but she couldn't be more opposite. So when Beau was trying to decide what type of vehicle to buy, she said, "Beau, just pray about it. I'll pray with you. But then after you pray, listen for God to answer."
"How am I supposed to know what he's saying?" Beau asked.
Katherine's response was, Just listen. Listen with your eyes, your hears, and your head. If the salesman calls and says he'll accept your terms, you'll know that's what God wants. And instead of thinking the salesman at the other dealership is rude and incompetent for not calling you back, hear that as God's answer that you aren't supposed to buy that truck."

Souls in Harmony

Beau looked at his wife and smiled, "I believe God answers prayers, but I'm ashamed to say I don't think about him using other people or situations like not getting a phone call to answer me."

Katherine reminded Beau of several decisions they'd made based on what she knew with full confidence to be God's answer to her prayers. Being reminded of these things gave Beau the perspective and boost of encouragement he needed to give his questions and thoughts to God and listen for his answer.

In a matter of a couple of days, God clearly Beau and Katherine's prayers about which vehicle to buy; giving Beau a sense of peace AND a huge boost of confidence in the power of prayer.

Beau's peace and confidence weren't based on getting the truck he wanted. They came from his new-found clarity and heightened sense of awareness of God's presence and concern with things big and small.

Since then, Beau and Katherine's prayer time together has grown to be one of the highlights of their day. They love praying and then talking about how they see and hear God answering them.

God is the Holy One. The Almighty. Creator and Master of the universe. But God is also our Father. He created us because he wanted to. He loved us even before we were born. I know that's incomprehensible to us, but it's true. And because he loves us, he wants to be in a relationship with us—a relationship where communication and closeness exists. When we have that kind of relationship with God, we are better able to receive and recognize the blessings he wants to share with us; including the blessing of marriage.

Week Thirty-two: Praying Your Way to Happiness

Prayer

Father in heaven, thank you for considering me worth listening to and worth talking to. Help me never take that for granted and never doubt that you are faithful to answer every prayer I pray. Give us the courage and wisdom to recognize the answers to my prayers and to know you always do what is best for me. Amen.

TASK 1 — WHAT NEEDS FOR YOUR SELF AND YOUR MARRIAGE DO YOU NEED TO TAKE BEFORE GOD?

_____
_____
_____
_____
_____
_____
_____
_____
_____
_____
_____
_____
_____
_____
_____
_____
_____
_____
_____
_____

Week Thirty-two: Praying Your Way to Happiness

TASK 2

WHAT DO YOU NEED TO SAY `THANK YOU´ TO GOD FOR THIS WEEK?

_____
_____
_____
_____
_____
_____
_____
_____
_____
_____
_____
_____
_____
_____
_____
_____
_____
_____
_____

TASK 3

WHAT ARE SOME WAYS YOU CAN MAKE PRAYER AND GOD MORE OF A FOCAL POINT OF YOUR MARRIAGE? WILL YOU?

_____
_____
_____
_____
_____
_____
_____
_____
_____
_____
_____
_____
_____
_____
_____
_____
_____

Week Thirty-two: Praying Your Way to Happiness

TASK 4

Stop and think about the prayers you have prayed over the last month. How has God answered those prayers? How did you receive the answers to your prayers?

_____
_____
_____
_____
_____
_____
_____
_____
_____
_____
_____
_____
_____
_____
_____
_____
_____
_____
_____
_____
_____
_____

TASK 5
MEMORIZE THIS WEEK'S VERSE.

Week Thirty-three: The Family Meeting

May the God of endurance and encouragement grant you to live in such harmony with one another, in accord with Christ Jesus, that together you may with one voice glorify the God and Father of our Lord Jesus Christ. ~Romans 15:5-6

"I was both angry and heartbroken when I heard my sister in-law tell my ten year-old niece to lie to her dad about the cost of a henna tattoo. She told her daughter that if her dad asked how much it cost, to say $20—not $50 (the actual cost). Not only was she teaching her daughter it is okay to lie, but she belittled my brother in-law's position as the head of the family, and essentially told her daughter it was okay to manipulate her dad. Seven years later this same girl turned teenager, is causing her parents one problem after another. I don't have to wonder why." ~Anita

Have you ever stopped to think about how different life would have been…

- If Eve would have talked things over with Adam before….
- If Abraham and Sarah would have talked things over with each other and prayed for patience to wait for God's timing to give them the son he promised, instead of taking matters into their own hands? Our world would be a very different (and more peaceful) place to live?
- If Laban wouldn't have been such a sneak, and Jacob would

have paid more attention to the woman he was getting ready to make love to on his (first) wedding night?
- If Samson and Delilah would have been honest with one another and if Delilah would have kept the outsiders out of her marriage (where they belonged)?
- If Ananias and Sapphira had talked about the right and wrong of what they planned to do and really thought things through?

When God says newlyweds are supposed to leave their parents and cleave to one another, he means for them to become a team…to communicate so they can work as a team.

When God says the two shall become one, he's not just talking about sex. He intends for couples to communicate, compromise, work together to find solutions and to make decisions together for the good of the marriage.

Living in harmony with one another and with your children takes work. Lots of work. And the first thing on the to-do list for living in harmony with your spouse should be honest communication. For example…

Don't say, "Nothing" instead of telling the truth when your spouse asks, "What's wrong?".

Don't hide price tags, say something cost less than it really did, or take that new sweater or golf club out of the closet a few weeks after you buy it and say, "I've had it for quite a while," when your spouse asks if it's new.

Tell your spouse where you are going, who you will be with, what you will be doing, and when you plan to be home.

Keep each other in the know about your individual schedules.

Don't ever say to your children, "Don't tell Dad/ Mom," "Let's just keep this between us," "This will be our secret so Mom/Dad doesn't get upset".

When you have a question, concern, need, or desire, speak up. You can't be mad at someone for not knowing what you don't tell them.

The lesson you need to learn from this week's devotion is that your marriage is serious business and like any successful business does, you need to have regular business meetings. Having a marriage/family 'business' meeting every week or every other week a great way to keep little things from becoming big things, and to prevent hurt feelings and problems from arising due to one of you being unaware of what's going on and what needs to be done.

Marriage/family meetings are the forum for problems to be discussed and to come up with viable solutions the two of you agree upon. They are also the forum for decisions to be made regarding work, money, family events, family schedules, and disagreements. Vacations can be planned and budgeted for, parenting dilemmas and differences of opinion can be resolved, and compromises can be reached for things like how much to spend for the holidays, where to spend the holidays, and whether or not you cut the cable.

A wedding is the coming together of two people. A marriage is the staying together of those two people. Marriage meetings is a way to make the staying together as amazing and wonderful as you want it, and God intends it to be.

Prayer

God, help us take our marriage seriously and to do all that we can not to take it or each other for granted. In Jesus' name, amen.

TASK 1
HAVE YOU EVER HAD A MARRIAGE MEETING? OR DO YOU JUST TAKE THINGS AS THEY COME?

_____
_____
_____
_____
_____
_____
_____
_____
_____
_____
_____
_____
_____
_____
_____
_____
_____
_____

Week Thirty-three: The Family Meeting

TASK 2
WHAT BENEFITS DO YOU SEE IN HAVING MARRIAGE MEETINGS?

TASK 3

SET A MARRIAGE MEETING TIME AND PLACE FOR THIS WEEK. MAKE A LIST OF THINGS YOU'D LIKE TO DISCUSS. OPEN AND CLOSE YOUR MEETING WITH PRAYER AND ALWAYS INCLUDE SOMETHING FUN—LIKE A DATING TRIVIA QUESTION OR MEMORY. SET A TIME FOR FUTURE MEETINGS AND STICK WITH THEM.

Week Thirty-three: The Family Meeting

Week Thirty-four: M & M's (Majors and Minors)

Know this, my beloved brothers: let every person be quick to hear, slow to speak, slow to anger. ~James 1:19

Morgan was twelve when her parents divorced, but she remembers the day they told her, and her brothers like it was yesterday. She couldn't believe the 'd' word was coming out of their mouths. They hadn't been fighting, and her dad didn't treat them badly like her friend Kim's dad did. They ate dinner together almost every night. They had a good time when they all went to the amusement park the week before school started. So what happened?

When Morgan asked her parents why they were getting a divorce, they looked at one another, then back and Morgan. It took a few seconds for her dad to finally answer, "Tires."
Morgan didn't think she'd heard correctly. Tires?
Yes, tires. Morgan's dad asked her mom to take her car to the tire shop to have new tires put on it. He pre-ordered them and made the appointment so it would mesh with his wife's schedule. When Morgan's mom arrived at the tire shop, she decided to swap out the tires her husband ordered for a cheaper option so that she could have the extra money to add to their Christmas budget—the budget they had already agreed upon. Morgan's dad noticed right away that the tires on the car weren't

the ones he had ordered. When he questioned his wife, she tried to skirt the issue, but eventually admitted what she'd done. From that day forward, broken trust, hurt feelings, resentment, and embarrassment over getting caught in a lie squeezed the life out of their marriage. Sounds crazy, right?

That's because it is. I think we'd all agree the lies and deceit were just flat-out wrong. And even though things escalated beyond the tire incident, when you stop to think about it, it really does all boil down to tires.

If Morgan's mom would have been honest and said she felt she needed or wanted more money for the Christmas budget, who is to say that wouldn't have happened? It wasn't so much that money was that tight, as it was the fact that together they had agreed to keep the Christmas spending within set limits.

So, what we have here is a textbook example of turning something minor into something major. What could have been resolved with a conversation and some give and take, ended up taking a marriage and family turning it into a statistic.

As husbands and wives, we MUST be CAREFUL not to let this happen in our marriages. We need to be constantly vigilant toward hearing and listening to our spouses. And not just with our ears. We need to listen with our eyes and our hearts. Don't expect your spouse to read your mind, and don't try to read theirs. Ask. Ask again. Be honest. Don't assume you know the answer or what the other is thinking. Don't be afraid to speak up. You are half of what matters in this marriage.

God's desire for your marriage is for you to work as a team. To trust one another. To honor one another. To respect and cherish one another. To be intimate and tender with one another. When any of those things is weak or missing, marriage doesn't work. Minor annoyances become irritants. Irritants become fuel for arguments. Arguments turn into major fights. Fights end in stalemates. And stalemates end in divorce.

Week Thirty-four: M & M's (Majors and Minors)

Both you and your spouse, as well as your children want, expect, and deserve more from your marriage than this. Don't you agree?

Prayer

LORD, make my spouse and I aware of the need for you, for honesty, transparency, and intimacy in our marriage. Help us understand and appreciate the fact that these things are what make a marriage God-strong and give us the desire to daily recommit to making our marriage what you want it to be. In Jesus' name, amen.

TASK 1 — WHAT MINOR ANNOYANCES AND FRUSTRATIONS ARE TUGGING AT YOUR MARRIAGE?

_____
_____
_____
_____
_____
_____
_____
_____
_____
_____
_____
_____
_____
_____
_____
_____
_____
_____

Week Thirty-four: M & M's (Majors and Minors)

TASK 2 — HOW DO YOU THINK THESE THINGS CAN BE RESOLVED?

TASK 3

WHEN HAVE YOU AND YOUR SPOUSE BEEN GUILTY OF TURNING A MINOR INTO A MAJOR? WHAT STEPS DID, OR ARE YOU TAKING TO RESOLVE THE SITUATION? OR IS IT STILL CREATING A BARRIER BETWEEN YOU? IF SO, COME TOGETHER AND PUT IT OUT THERE FOR THE PURPOSE OF RESOLVING THE ISSUE AND REINFORCING THE FOUNDATION OF YOUR MARRIAGE.

TASK 4

WHAT, IF ANY, ISSUES ARE YOU DEALING WITH RIGHT NOW THAT MIGHT POSSIBLY GO FROM A MINOR TO A MAJOR? GET THESE THINGS OUT IN THE OPEN NOW, SO THAT YOU NEVER HAVE TO ANSWER THE QUESTION OF 'WHAT HAPPENED' BY SAYING, "TIRES".

_____
_____
_____
_____
_____
_____
_____
_____
_____
_____
_____
_____
_____
_____
_____
_____
_____
_____
_____
_____

Souls in Harmony

Week Thirty-five: Change it Up

Finally, brothers, whatever is true, whatever is honorable, whatever is just, whatever is pure, whatever is lovely, whatever is commendable, if there is any excellence, if there is anything worthy of praise, think about these things. ~Philippians 4:8

It's easy to complain, isn't it? We live in such a negative society, that complaining has become not second, but first nature to us. Think about it—did you ever hear your parents or grandparents use the term 'road rage'? Did you ever witness them having road rage? Did the notion ever enter your parents' or your mind that someone might come to your school and start shooting at people? And what about the fact that we didn't use to leave scathing reviews of various businesses, shows like "Judge Judy" and "People's Court" were inconceivable a generation or two ago, and bullying led to a black eye instead of suicide?

So, what happened? How did we get from a society in which places like Mayberry, Walton's Mountain, and the Tanner house weren't fiction and fantasy, to…this?

The most direct answer to that question, is we stopped including Jesus. We made Jesus and God an option instead of a necessity. But let's not leave it there. Let's look at the problem from the viewpoint of our relationships with each other.

What happened is that instead of one on one conversations

and yes, even confrontations, we have become a society that grumbles and complains either internally or behind the walls of cyberspace and selfishness. We would rather complain than put forth the effort to fix something or make amends. We would rather bash and ridicule someone's character instead of getting to know them, showing empathy and compassion, or just being nice. We would rather demand our rights instead of enjoying our privileges. We would rather criticize and make others feel small instead of trying to see things from their point of view and conceding that we might actually be wrong once in a while, or that our way isn't always the best or only way.

At this point you might be wondering why the 'soapbox speech' about the negativity of society. If so, you can stop wondering, because here it is: you are part of our negative society. You, your spouse, and pretty much everyone else, have become complainers and whiners instead of communicators and fixers. And just so you know, it's not working very well.

As marriage partners, we are supposed to not only look for the good in our spouse, we are supposed to nurture it, recognize it, appreciate it, take joy in it, honor it, respect it…. Get the point? But we're not—not always, anyway. If we were, then Christian marriages wouldn't be imploding at the same rate as non-Christian marriages.

People, it's time to stop hiding behind complaints about your marriage and start changing those things into something good and positive. It's time to stop hiding behind 'he or she won't, doesn't, or isn't', and focus on who YOU are and what you do and what you bring to the marriage. Oh, and then make the changes that need to be made!

Change—it doesn't have to be bad, scary, or even radical. Often times in a marriage, the little changes make the biggest improvements. So…

- If you don't like the fact that your wife spends $100 a month

to get her nails done, ask her to come up with an alternative.
- If you want to stay home with the kids but think you husband won't want the stress of being the sole provider or want to change your lifestyle to fit the reduced income, don't harbor resentment based on assumptions. Talk about it and come up with a solution together.
- If you want to gag just thinking about eating beef stroganoff one more time, say so. There are plenty of other options for dinnertime.
- If you feel your sex life has reached the point of being too predictable or mechanical, tell your spouse you would like to spice things up. Be sure you let them know you aren't bored or tired of them, but that you want to take things up a notch and decide together what you both feel comfortable with trying.
- Are you bored with your weekend routine or Friday nights nodding off to sleep in front of the tv? Invite friends over once a month or so. Play cards or board games. Look at old picture albums together. Whatever—just change things up a weekend at a time and see what happens.
- Are you panicking at the thought of spending another holiday with your in-laws? Talk it over and come up with a plan to change things around that will give you the relief you need AND keep extended family members (somewhat) happy.

Do you see what can and should happen here? Instead of thinking about your marriage in terms of being stuck, think of it as your life's adventure. Remember that it is what YOU make it, so make it true, noble, right, good, lovely, admirable, and all those things God promises will fill our hearts, souls, and minds with the peace of fulfilling contentment.

Week Thirty-five: Change it Up

PRAYER

LORD, open my eyes to what I need to do to be a better person and better spouse. Give me the courage, wisdom, and determination to change and to do it with the right spirit. Amen.

Souls in Harmony

TASK 1 — WHAT CHANGES WOULD YOU LIKE TO MAKE IN YOUR MARRIAGE?

_____
_____
_____
_____
_____
_____
_____
_____
_____
_____
_____
_____
_____
_____
_____
_____
_____
_____
_____
_____

Week Thirty-five: Change it Up

TASK 2 — WHAT CHANGES DO YOU NEED TO MAKE IN YOURSELF?

TASK 3
HOW WOULD MAKING THESE CHANGES MAKE YOU A BETTER PERSON? MAKE YOUR MARRIAGE BETTER?

TASK 4 — WHAT IS KEEPING YOU FROM MAKING THESE CHANGES?

_____
_____
_____
_____
_____
_____
_____
_____
_____
_____
_____
_____
_____
_____
_____
_____
_____
_____
_____
_____

Souls in Harmony

TASK 5

PICK TWO OF THE CHANGES YOU LISTED (ONE IN YOURSELF AND ONE IN YOUR MARRIAGE). START WORKING ON THEM TODAY. ONCE YOU FEEL YOU ARE ON SOLID GROUND WITH THEM, MOVE ON TO THE NEXT TWO.....

_____
_____
_____
_____
_____
_____
_____
_____
_____
_____
_____
_____
_____
_____
_____
_____
_____
_____
_____

Week Thirty-six: Eewww, Yuk!

Let him kiss me with the kisses of his mouth! For your love is better than wine. ~Song of Solomon 1:2

When the kids were small and even when they were teenagers, they would laugh, scrunch their nose and say, "Eewww, gross!", or "Get a room" when John and I would kiss or say something romantic, aka 'mushy' to each other. We were never inappropriate, of course, but kids think anything is weird or 'gross' when it comes to their parents and stuff like that.

We'd smile and laugh and tell them it was a good thing we love each other. And once they were teenager, John liked to tease them by asking, "Well, how do you think you got here?" That, of course, led to another chorus of "Eewww, gross!"
But now that they are grown and have kids of their own, they have actually said how glad they are for those displays of affection. They said that even though they didn't act like it, those little acts of PDA made them feel safe. Secure. Happy. Loved. ~Jackie
Your children need to know you love their mom/dad. They need to see it. Feel it. Hear it. And here are more than a few reasons why…
Knowing your parents love one another makes a child feel safe and secure. Unafraid.
Knowing your parents love one another gives a child confidence and a healthier self-esteem.

Souls in Harmony

Knowing your parents love one another gives a child a healthy example of what male/female relationships should look like.

Knowing your parents love one another gives a child a model for their own marriage and greatly reduces the chances of an abusive or unhealthy marriage.

Knowing your parents love one another reduces the chances of a child trying to 'play' divide and conquer with his/her parents.

Knowing your parents love each other reduces the chances of premarital sex, promiscuity, and unplanned pregnancy during the child's teenage years.

You do the math—that's six extremely good reasons for appropriate PDA in front of your kids. But what's appropriate? Hugs, handholding, kissing (not too heavy), patting or pinching on the bum, cuddling, romantic (not sexually charged) comments, and spooning.

If you stop and think about it, why wouldn't you want your children to know how much you love your spouse?

PRAYER

Father in heaven, you show your love for us in so many ways; giving me the security and sense of confidence and self-worth I need. Help us give that to our children, as well, by giving them a healthy view of our love for one another. In Jesus' name, amen.

Week Thirty-six: Eewww, Yuk!

TASK 1

IF YOUR CHILDREN WERE ASKED THE QUESTION, "HOW DO YOU KNOW MOMMY AND DADDY LOVE EACH OTHER?" WHAT WOULD THEY SAY?

_____
_____
_____
_____
_____
_____
_____
_____
_____
_____
_____
_____
_____
_____
_____
_____
_____
_____
_____

Souls in Harmony

TASK 2
HOW OFTEN DO YOU AND YOUR SPOUSE SHOW AFFECTION OUTSIDE THE BEDROOM?

Week Thirty-six: Eewww, Yuk!

TASK 3
WHAT DO YOU DO TO SHOW YOUR LOVE AND AFFECTION TO ONE ANOTHER?

_____
_____
_____
_____
_____
_____
_____
_____
_____
_____
_____
_____
_____
_____
_____
_____
_____
_____

Souls in Harmony

TASK 4 IF YOU STILL HAVE CHILDREN AT HOME, BETWEEN THE AGES OF 4 AND 18, SPEND SOME TIME GOING THROUGH YOUR WEDDING PICTURES AS A FAMILY AND TALK ABOUT YOUR DATING RELATIONSHIP, YOUR WEDDING, AND THE EARLY (PRE-KID) YEARS OF YOUR MARRIAGE.

_____
_____
_____
_____
_____
_____
_____
_____
_____
_____
_____
_____
_____
_____
_____
_____
_____
_____

Week Thirty-six: Eewww, Yuk!

Week Thirty-seven: Trading Places

So whatever you wish that others would do to you, do also to them, for this is the Law and the Prophets. ~Matthew 7:12

If you have kids, of if you were once a kid yourself, you have undoubtedly 'met' the Berenstain Bears. And if you know very much at all about the bear family that lives in the treehouse down the sunny dirt road deep in Bear Country, then you know they have quite a knack for teaching life-lessons that stick with you for a long, long time.

Among the many life-lessons they teach is appreciation for others, i.e. putting yourself in someone else's shoes. In other words, trading places with someone so that you get an up-close-and-personal view of what it takes to be 'them'. In the case of the Berenstain Bears' "Trouble With Grownups", Momma and Papa Bear taught the cubs an important lesson in respecting other people's feelings, jobs, and authority.
We don't have any problem recognizing how important that is when it comes to parents and children, law enforcement and the public, teachers and students, and employers and employees, but what about the roles of husbands and wives? How often do you really stop to think about what it's like to be your spouse and to have the responsibilities in your marriage and home that they have?

Souls in Harmony

Granted, the roles these days are considerably less line-in-the-sand-ish, than they were even a generation or two ago. But even taking that into consideration, every marriage has a 'system' for running smoothly based on jobs or responsibilities divided up (so to speak) between the husband and the wife. And let me just say that in a Christian marriage, those roles should be more defined than they usually are in non-Christian marriages. So, the next time you start thinking he/she doesn't appreciate, respect, or understand you, tell him/her how you are feeling. And instead of doing things that make your spouse feel unappreciated, disrespected, and misunderstood, put the Golden Rule in high gear and be for your spouse the person you want them to be for you.

Phrases like, "He doesn't understand," "She thinks I'm just off having fun," "He doesn't want a wife, he wants a mom," "She acts like she's some kind of martyr or saint," "How hard can it be," "He works more than he has to so he doesn't have to come home," "She's a mom—she's supposed to be able to do all those things," should NEVER cross your lips. Should NEVER be what you think on or harbor in your heart.

These things have no place in a marriage where Godly leadership, submission, and partnership are meant to be. Instead…

- Wives should be grateful for husbands who take on the bulk of responsibility for shepherding, supporting, and leading your family.
- Wives should be willing to put themselves in the care and protection of their husbands, and husbands should willingly and wholeheartedly fulfill these responsibilities.
- Wives should communicate their thoughts and feelings and listen as their husband does the same.
- Husbands should be sensitive to the needs of their wives by sharing in parenting responsibilities as equally as possible, by communicating their intentions, by not adding to the

Week Thirty-seven: Trading Places

burden of household duties, but rather helping with them, and by acknowledging and respecting his wife's need for personal time and space.
- Husbands should take their role as head of household seriously, by being involved and invested in the household.
- Husbands should honor their wives by expressing gratitude and respect for all they do to keep the family and household together.

It doesn't matter how traditional or non-traditional your marriage is when it comes to how much money each spouse makes, what their job is, who does the cleaning, cooking, and yardwork. Leadership, submission, and teamwork as defined and directed by God are essential for a solid and happy marriage.

PRAYER

God, make me more grateful and appreciative of what we do for one another. Help us to build one another up and encourage one another in our God-given roles. In Jesus' name, amen.

TASK 1 SET ASIDE FIFTEEN MINUTES OR SO TO TELL ONE ANOTHER HOW MUCH YOU APPRECIATE WHAT THEY BRING TO THE MARRIAGE AND TO YOUR HOUSEHOLD.

_____
_____
_____
_____
_____
_____
_____
_____
_____
_____
_____
_____
_____
_____
_____
_____

Week Thirty-seven: Trading Places

TASK 2 — WHAT RESPONSIBILITIES, IF ANY, WOULD YOU LIKE YOUR SPOUSE TO RELIEVE YOU FROM? TALK ABOUT THESE THINGS AND COME UP WITH A PLAN YOU ARE BOTH HAPPY WITH.

_____
_____
_____
_____
_____
_____
_____
_____
_____
_____
_____
_____
_____
_____
_____
_____
_____
_____
_____
_____
_____
_____

TASK 3
WHAT ARE SOME THINGS YOU CAN DO TO BE MORE SUPPORTIVE AND APPRECIATIVE OF YOUR SPOUSE'S ROLES AND RESPONSIBILITIES?

_____
_____
_____
_____
_____
_____
_____
_____
_____
_____
_____
_____
_____
_____
_____
_____
_____
_____

Week Thirty-seven: Trading Places

Week Thirty-eight: Let's Talk...No, Let's Really Talk

A gentle tongue is a tree of life, but perverseness in it breaks the spirit. ~Proverbs 15:4

Andrew and Abby are childhood sweethearts who married right out of high school. Now in their mid-twenties, they have two little girls, are faithful and committed to the LORD and one another, and could easily teach couples young and old the art and importance of talking to one another.

They don't just talk about the kids, trying to decide where they want to request their next duty station to be (Andrew is in the military), when the car needs an oil change, or whether or not Abby and the girls will temporarily move closer to her parents while he's deployed. No, they talk about everything. Movies, the grocery list, what the kids did at the park, the weather, the sermon they heard at church on Sunday, their daily devotional time together, how Abby wants to decorate the bathroom, the new recruits….you name it, they talk about it.

And then there's William and Mary Ruth. William isn't much for conversation just for the sake of talking. He thinks that when people are talking, they need to be making a decision, sharing important news, complaining about something, telling an interesting story, or imparting wisdom or instruction of some sort. But talking just to visit? To him, that's a waste of time. Mary Ruth, on the other hand, loves to chit chat. But to try to do so with her husband, whom she dearly loves, is painful at best.

"We can literally ride in a car for hours at a time without him saying a word. It drives me nuts! Sometimes I want to say something I know he will argue with me about just so he'll talk. Over the years I've tried lots of things, but he just rolls his eyes and says he doesn't have anything to say," Mary Ruth sighs, before adding, "Then when he does decide to talk, he expects my undivided attention. But I have to be honest, after forty years of the silent treatment, I'm not all that interested in what he has to say. Why should I listen to him talk at me when he doesn't ever want to listen or talk to me.?"

Go, Andrew and Abby! You're doing great and God is well-pleased with you. William and Mary Ruth's situation… heartbreaking. William wouldn't have to be Mr. Chatty, but would it hurt him to engage in casual conversation? Who knows (we all do) what a positive change it would make in his marriage and other relationships, as well!

Conversations, deep and otherwise, are something we all need. God created that need within us, so to deny it, is to be less than who we are meant (created) to be. There's an argument for you! Talking is part of your purpose. Talking works to complete you. I like that—don't you?

As marriage partners, you can't truly be partners if you don't communicate. It doesn't matter if you've been married two… seven…fifteen…or even forty years—if you don't talk to one another, you cannot really know one another. As marriage partners you need to talk about:
- What you did throughout the day.
- What the kids and grandkids are up to
- Your plans with friends, serving or fellowship at church, and so forth

Week Thirty-eight: Let's Talk…No, Let's Really Talk

- Concerns about family, the house, financial matters, work, church, your community, and whatever else is on your mind
- How to parent
- How to interact with your parents and extended family members
- A plan for retirement
- What to do in the event of your parents needing to be cared for
- How you want health issues to be handled
- Financial planning
- Your will and estate planning
- Fears
- Wants and needs
- What makes you laugh and what makes you cry
- Household projects
- What you don't like about yourself and your spouse (be nice)
- Taking a moral stand in an immoral world
- Career goals and struggles
- Work-related issues
- Things that tempt you
- Spiritual questions and musings
- Encouragements you find in reading scripture
- Your love, admiration, and appreciation for one another
- Your friend relationships
- Politics (Yikes!)

That's quite a list, isn't it? That's the point. You should be willing to talk about anything and everything. No, you should be more than willing. You should be willfully (intentionally) talking about these things…and more.

And one last thing—don't just talk these things over with each other. Talk them over with God, too.

Prayer

God, open my mouth, my ears, my heart, and my mind to hear my spouse, to speak to my spouse, so that we can know you and know each other fully. Help me enjoy talking and sharing with my spouse and help us come together to be the team you desire us to be. In Jesus' name, amen.

TASK 1

WHAT GRADE WOULD YOU GIVE YOUR MARRIAGE WHEN IT COMES TO TALKING BEYOND WHAT IS NECESSARY?

TASK 2: HOW SATISFIED ARE YOU WITH THE AMOUNT AND DEPTH OF CONVERSATION BETWEEN YOU AND YOUR SPOUSE?

_____
_____
_____
_____
_____
_____
_____
_____
_____
_____
_____
_____
_____
_____
_____
_____
_____
_____

Week Thirty-eight: Let's Talk…No, Let's Really Talk

TASK 3　IF TALKING ISN'T A STRONGPOINT IN YOUR MARRIAGE, WHY DO YOU THINK THAT IS?

_____
_____
_____
_____
_____
_____
_____
_____
_____
_____
_____
_____
_____
_____
_____
_____
_____
_____
_____

TASK 4: WHAT WOULD YOU LIKE TO DO TO MAKE YOUR MARRIAGE MORE CONVERSATIONAL?

_____
_____
_____
_____
_____
_____
_____
_____
_____
_____
_____
_____
_____
_____
_____
_____
_____
_____
_____
_____

Week Thirty-eight: Let's Talk…No, Let's Really Talk

TASK 5
EACH OF YOU NEED TO CHOOSE TWO TOPICS FROM THE LIST YOU'VE JUST READ. SET ASIDE AT LEAST TWENTY MINUTES ONE EVENING/MORNING (WHENEVER IS BEST FOR YOU) TO TALK ABOUT ONE OF THE FOUR.

Yes, that means you will spend twenty minutes four times this week having a meaningful conversation with your spouse. Remember: these conversations will not always and should not always be used to solve problems or make decisions. Sometimes it really is a great thing to talk just to talk and share what is on your heart and mind.

_____
_____
_____
_____
_____
_____
_____
_____
_____
_____
_____
_____
_____
_____
_____

Week Thirty-nine: The Best Things in Life Aren't Things

Do not store up for yourselves treasures on earth, where moths and vermin destroy, and where thieves break in and steal. But store up for yourselves treasures in heaven, where moths and vermin do not destroy, and where thieves do not break in and steal. For where your treasure is, there your heart will be also. ~Matthew 6:19-21

A friend of mine took an informal poll, i.e. she asked her social media contacts, what their most prized possession was. There were (sadly) a few people who responded by saying their $500 purse, their house, the desk in their office because it represents being in charge, and even their dog. But those were the exceptions. The overwhelming majority of people responded with things like… My Grandma's cake pan and recipes because it keeps me connected to her. The minute I touch them, I smell her kitchen. The fishing pole my dad taught me to fish with. The music box my dad got for me while he was deployed. The Christmas treetop angle my son made in Sunday school when he was two. I can still see his smile and twinkling eyes when I told him we would put it on top of our tree forever (and I will). A partial bottle of my grandpa's aftershave. It's the one he was using when he passed away. Thirty-five years later I still open it once in a while just so I can smell that comforting, familiar smell. It makes me feel safe and loved.

Do you see the difference? The things most people claimed as their most prized possessions had little or nothing to do with the item itself. It was about the person and the memories associated with them. It's the tangible representing the intangible. This is something you need to remember in your marriage—that the things you give one another aren't what matters. It's the memories you make together and what you do for and with one another that matters. Trust me, unless you are one of those housewives of such and such a place couples, your wife would much rather have you home for dinner and to help with the kids' homework than for you to work the hours necessary to have a fancy house to eat dinner and do homework in. You also need to know that your husband would much rather have a note scribbled on a piece of junk mail tucked into his lunch, his suitcase, or gym bag instead of just about anything. Why? Because it says you care about staying connected even when you are apart. When Solomon wrote in the book of Ecclesiastes, that the end of a matter is better than the beginning, I think to some extent that he was talking about the importance of making memories and grasping the truth that relationships are what matters…not things. He was reminding us not to waste our time here on accumulating, but instead, to focus on associating; nurturing relationships and making memories. Are you ready to take Solomon's advice?

Prayer

God, thank you for memories—both good and bad. Thank you for the good ones because they remind me of the many blessings I've been given. Thank you for the bad ones that remind me how much better life is when I live it for you, and to teach me to trust you more. Amen.

TASK 1
WHAT ARE YOUR MOST TREASURED MEMORIES AND WHAT THINGS DO YOU ASSOCIATE WITH THOSE MEMORIES?

_____
_____
_____
_____
_____
_____
_____
_____
_____
_____
_____
_____
_____
_____
_____
_____
_____

Week Thirty-nine: The Best Things in Life Aren't Things

TASK 2
WHAT SOUNDS AND SMELLS CONJURE UP PLEASANT MEMORIES FOR YOU?

_____
_____
_____
_____
_____
_____
_____
_____
_____
_____
_____
_____
_____
_____
_____
_____
_____
_____
_____
_____

TASK 3 SPEND SOME TIME WITH YOUR SPOUSE RECALLING YOUR MOST SPECIAL, FUNNY, SCARY, AND SAD MEMORIES OF YOUR LIFE TOGETHER. TALK ABOUT HOW THE EVENTS THAT MADE THESE MEMORIES AFFECTED YOUR RELATIONSHIP.

_____
_____
_____
_____
_____
_____
_____
_____
_____
_____
_____
_____
_____
_____
_____
_____
_____
_____
_____

Week Thirty-nine: The Best Things in Life Aren't Things

TASK 4
WHAT ARE SOME THINGS YOU CAN AND WILL DO TO CREATE MORE MEMORIES TOGETHER?

_____
_____
_____
_____
_____
_____
_____
_____
_____
_____
_____
_____
_____
_____
_____
_____
_____
_____
_____

Week Forty: I'm...sorry

So if you are offering your gift at the altar and there remember that your brother has something against you, leave your gift there before the altar and go. First be reconciled to your brother, and then come and offer your gift. ~Matthew 5:23-24

Darren has worked as a correction's officer (prison guard) for nearly twenty years. The nature of his job makes him more suspicious than most people. He tends to demand instead of asking and extends little or no flexibility and grace when it comes to rules and expectations. Not just at work—at home, too.

Darren is a Christian, but his strict and rigid personality often conflict with God's expectations for him as a husband, father, and spiritual leader of their home. This is especially obvious when it comes to apologizing to his wife, Annette, and their twins, for putting unreasonable and unfair expectations and restrictions on them. Darren never apologizes for his words or actions. Never. He is of the mindset that if he no longer brings the matter up, it's over and that should be good enough.
It's not.
Annette loves her husband, and she does her best to extend grace and understanding to him, because she knows it cannot be easy to 'take off' his professional persona and exchange it for his husband and dad persona. She knows the stark contrast between the two is bound to bleed over sometimes. But it isn't

easy, because from where she is standing, Darren doesn't feel she or their twins mean enough to him to express remorse for bringing too much of his work self into their home, is hurtful and has caused her to build up a pretty big reserve of resentment. And the twins, who are getting ready to become teenagers, want very little to do with their dad these days.

A few weeks ago, Annette told her best friend she needed prayer—that her marriage and family needed prayer…and lots of it. She accidentally let an ink pen go through the washer and dryer; ruining one of Darren's uniforms.

"It wasn't like I did it on purpose," she said, "but when I apologized, Darren actually had the nerve to say that an apology wasn't worth much—that it didn't fix the ruined uniform."

Then in tears, she finished by telling her friend, "I just looked at him and said that the kids and I would give anything for an apology from you now and then and that just hearing him say the words I'm sorry would make our home a much happier place to be. Then I turned around and left. And quite honestly, I don't know that I want to go back."

What happens with Darren and Annette remains to be seen, but unfortunately, they are not alone. A lot of people have difficulty saying, "I'm sorry". They'll find any excuse they can to avoid it. But why? We all make mistakes, so why not just own it and move on? And just because you don't mean to hurt of offend someone is no guarantee you don't. So instead of putting the blame onto them by saying they are too sensitive or whatever, just apologize and move on.

The Bible very plainly states that we are to treat others the way we want to be treated, that husbands and wives are to respect each other, and that the relationship is supposed to mirror that of Jesus and the Church. There is no room in any of these instructions for ignoring the hurt you bring to your spouse. None. At. All.

Souls in Harmony

When you love someone—really love someone with the 1st Corinthians 13 love God calls us to have, not apologizing isn't on the radar. No matter what you do for a living or other excuse you try to give. That isn't love. So if you say you love your spouse, prove it by never being too proud or too selfish to say, "I'm sorry".

Prayer

LORD, humble my heart to be remorseful for those things I do that hurt my spouse. Open my heart and mind to see the need to apologize for these things and ask his/her forgiveness. I love him/her and want to be the husband/wife he/she deserves. In your name I pray, amen.

TASK 1 — DO YOU HAVE TROUBLE SAYING, "I'M SORRY"? WHY OR WHY NOT?

TASK 2

DO YOU THINK IT IS IMPORTANT TO VERBALLY APOLOGIZE, OR DO ACTIONS SPEAK LOUDER THAN WORDS? EXPLAIN.

_____
_____
_____
_____
_____
_____
_____
_____
_____
_____
_____
_____
_____
_____
_____
_____
_____

Week Forty: I'm…sorry

TASK 3
WHAT DO YOU NEED TO APOLOGIZE TO YOUR SPOUSE ABOUT? MAKE A POINT TO DO SO AS SOON AS POSSIBLE.

_____
_____
_____
_____
_____
_____
_____
_____
_____
_____
_____
_____
_____
_____
_____
_____
_____
_____
_____
_____

Souls in Harmony

Week Forty-one: You Are My Everything

Did he not make them one, with a portion of the Spirit in their union? And what was the one God seeking? Godly offspring. So guard yourselves in your spirit, and let none of you be faithless to the wife of your youth. ~Malachi 2:15

When we hear words like faithless, unfaithful, or infidelity, we automatically think in terms of sex. Why wouldn't we? The terms certainly apply, don't they? But there is more than one way to be unfaithful to your spouse. Anything you do or don't do that hampers intimacy or that takes the place of intimacy with your spouse is a form of infidelity and faithlessness.

- Putting your career in front of your marriage
- Giving your friends, extended family, or even your children ahead of your marriage
- 'Losing' yourself in a hobby
- Becoming too absorbed with the kids
- Hiding behind insecurities
- Unresolved issues, resentment, and anger
- Unforgiveness

Each of these things is capable of filling the space in your marriage intended for intimacy. And since every single one of us deals with these issues, we need to know how to be proactive in protecting our marriage. We need to be able to wake up each morning with the mindset that the person you are married to is your everything.

Providing for your family—whether working a 9 to 5, working from home, or working as a stay at home mom—is essential. But when you let that 9 to 5 become an 8 to 7, when you bring your work home with you, when you are more concerned with the doing and the outcome than you are the 'why'—your career is squashing your intimacy factor. Always or usually choosing friends, extended family, or kids over your spouse is both hurtful and harmful. Speaking negatively about your spouse to friends, your children, and extended family breaks the bonds of intimacy in your marriage. No, this doesn't mean your infant and toddler shouldn't have their near-constant needs met. This also doesn't mean you can't have a social life without your spouse with your friends that are the same sex as you are. And no, this doesn't mean Monday evening coffee and dessert with your mom and sisters you've enjoyed since you were a teenager has to end.

The Bible provides numerous examples of close relationships between friends and extended family members—David and Jonathan, Paul, Barnabas, and Timothy, Jesus, Peter, James, and John, Elijah and Elisha, to name a few. Zelophehad's daughters shared a close relationship, Ruth and Naomi were extremely close, and Esther's bond with her adopted father wasn't diminished after she became a queen. You see, it's not about excluding everything and everyone else from your life—it's about making each other number one…after God, of course.

Prayer

God, help me see the need for intimacy in marriage and help me make it a priority. I love my husband/wife, but in some ways, I have let self and the busy-ness of doing life take up more space than the person I am sharing life with. Help me want more of 'us' and less of everything else. In the name of Jesus, amen.

Week Forty-one: You Are My Everything

TASK 1

WOULD YOUR SPOUSE SAY YOU PUT ANY OF THE THINGS LISTED AS BEING 'INTIMACY STEALERS' IN FRONT OF THEM? WHICH ONES, AND WHY?

_____
_____
_____
_____
_____
_____
_____
_____
_____
_____
_____
_____
_____
_____
_____
_____
_____
_____
_____
_____

TASK 2 WHAT CHANGES CAN YOU MAKE TO RESOLVE THIS PROBLEM?

_____
_____
_____
_____
_____
_____
_____
_____
_____
_____
_____
_____
_____
_____
_____
_____
_____
_____

Week Forty-one: You Are My Everything

TASK 3 ARE YOU WILLING TO MAKE THEM? WHY OR WHY NOT?

TASK 4
SPEND TIME PRAYING TOGETHER FOR A MORE INTIMATE RELATIONSHIP.

___

Week Forty-one: You Are My Everything

TASK 5

Spend a few minutes every night this week at bedtime cuddling. If it leads to more...fine. If not, that's okay, too. Just knowing you end the day in each other's arms is special.

Souls in Harmony

Week Forty-two: More Than Just Roommates

Then the Lord God said, "It is not good that the man should be alone; I will make him a helper fit for him." ~Genesis 2:18

A preacher doing a series on marriage stood in front of his congregation one Sunday and asked, "Are you married or are you roommates?" He then went on to explain the differences between the two, how dangerous it is for husbands and wives to let their marriages lapse into roommate status, and what couples should do to protect their marriage from this sad state of disrepair.

What about you? Have you ever stopped to think about just how married you are? Are you intimate? Is he/she the one you want to confide in? Laugh with? Cuddle with? Ask for help? Is he/she the one you want to tell news to first? Does their touch give you that warm feeling inside? Or are you more like roommates or business partners? Do your conversations consist of little to nothing more than covering the kids' schedules, reminders to pick up the dry cleaning, conferring about bills, complaining about the neighbors, and debates over what color to paint the front porch?

Do you see the difference?

Jill and Aaron are childhood sweethearts, the parents of four grown children, and recently celebrated their 39th wedding anniversary. They appear to have a happy, healthy marriage, but the truth of the matter is, they are little more than roommates. It hasn't always been that way, but years of Aaron's resistance to talk just to talk and not leaving his work at work, have taken their toll.

But now that he's retired, Aaron is ready to be different…better, which is great. Or it would be, if Jill was able to let go of the past. After 30 years of near-silence and stoicism, she's made her own little world, so to speak, and it was one she is comfortable in. She wants a better marriage, but Aaron's assumptive attitude seems a lot like just another one of his my-way-or-the-highway decisions.

These two are clearly roommates. Hopefully, though, they can find their way back to being married…soon.

Proverbs 17:1 says, "Better a dry crust with peace and quiet than a house full of feasting, with strife." The peace and quiet Solomon is talking about here is the kind that comes from being helpmates. Connected partners. Husbands and wives. It's the peace and quiet that happens when you deliberately and consistently put your marriage second only to God. It's the peace and quiet that comes when you decide every single day to be a husband or a wife instead of a roommate/business partner. You can do business with just about anyone. You can discuss the weather with total strangers, you can share recipes or talk sports with coworkers, the neighbors, or parents of kids on your daughter's swim team. But marriage—that's something else altogether different and better.

TASK 1 MAKE IT A NON-NEGOTIABLE TO SPEND TIME TOGETHER TALKING ABOUT CURRENT EVENTS, SOMETHING FUNNY YOU SAW/HEARD, OR FOND MEMORIES OF THE PAST. DO THIS AT LEAST TWICE A WEEK.

___

___

___

___

___

___

___

___

___

___

___

___

___

___

___

___

___

___

___

Week Forty-two: More Than Just Roommates

TASK 2
GO ON DATES. HOLD HANDS. SIT CLOSE TOGETHER. GO PARKING.

TASK 3

WHAT WERE YOUR TOP THREE THINGS YOU ENJOYED DOING WITH YOUR SPOUSE WHEN YOU WERE DATING. DO THEM AGAIN.

___

Week Forty-two: More Than Just Roommates

TASK 4
Read at least a book a month and tell your spouse about it.

_____
_____
_____
_____
_____
_____
_____
_____
_____
_____
_____
_____
_____
_____
_____
_____
_____
_____
_____
_____

TASK 5 GET A KID'S JOKE BOOK OR LAFFY TAFFY CANDY. LAUGH AT THE SILLINESS OF THE PUNCHLINES.

TASK 6 HAVE A NERF WAR, SILLY STRING FIGHT, OR WATER GUN SHOOTOUT.

_____
_____
_____
_____
_____
_____
_____
_____
_____
_____
_____
_____
_____
_____
_____
_____
_____
_____

Week Forty-two: More Than Just Roommates

TASK 7
SURPRISE YOUR SPOUSE WITH LITTLE TREATS (FROYO, FLOWERS, FAVORITE SNACK, BREAKFAST IN BED....)

Week Forty-three: Me Days

Beloved, I pray that all may go well with you and that you may be in good health, as it goes well with your soul. ~3rd John 1:2

'Me time', as the not-so-original name implies, is the time I take just for me. Sometimes I take an entire day, sometimes it's a thirty minute walk with just me and possibly the dog, sometimes it's piddling in the flowerbeds and garden where I can think and ponder my thoughts with God knowing no one is going to offer to help pull weeds, and sometimes it's lunch and conversation with a friend. No husband, kids, or grandkids. Just me and someone who doesn't want anything from me but conversation and friendship. My 'me time' keeps me from getting lost in other titles and feeling like I don't matter. ~Phyllis
I take some time every day just for me. Sometimes it's twenty minutes. Sometimes it's a few hours. It's not so much about how much time, but how I spend it. Reading, walking, browsing through Pintrest and deciding what I'm gonna try next, even grocery shopping by myself is a treat sometimes. I also encourage my husband to do things by himself sometimes, too. He doesn't seem to need or want as much of that as I do, but when he takes it, he admits it's nice to not have to do anything other than what he wants to do. Silence and solitude aren't bad. They are refreshing—when kept in perspective and seen as times of renewal, not hiding. ~Carly
Each year I take two week-long hunting trips with my brothers, my son, and two of my uncles. No, I'm not

alone, but it's still what I consider personal time. No talk about household chores, no work, no deciding what to eat for dinner—just relaxing and being together. ~Preston

Once or twice a month I take a few hours to hop in my motorcycle and just ride some backroads to relax and just be alone in my thoughts. It clears my head and helps me put things in a more proper perspective. And when I'm better as a person, everything else in my life is better, too. ~John

You've heard that little song about the knee bone being connected to the shin bone and the shin bone being connected to the foot bone, and on and on and on. And it's true—every part of us is connected to another part. We are, as scripture states in 1st Corinthians 12:12, individuals made up of many parts. What that little song doesn't tell us, though, is that it's about more than just our bones. Psalm 139 is one you are likely familiar with—especially verses 13-16. But if you start reading a few verses before that, you will see that God doesn't see our physical bodies as separate from the emotional, mental, and spiritual aspects of who we are. And because God doesn't view these things separately, neither should we. Let's look at what David wrote to God when he realized this simple, yet profound truth…

You have searched me, Lord, and you know me. You know when I sit and when I rise; you perceive my thoughts from afar. You discern my going out and my lying down; you are familiar with all my ways. Before a word is on my tongue you, Lord, know it completely…For you created my inmost being; you knit me together in my mother's womb. I praise you because I am fearfully and wonderfully made; your works are wonderful; I know that full well. My frame was not hidden from you when I was made in the secret place, when I was woven together in the depths of the earth. Your eyes saw my unformed body; all the days ordained for me were written in your book before one of them came to be. ~Psalm 139:1-4 and 13-16

Taking 'me time' like Phyllis and the others do, is essential for your personal wellbeing, as well as for the wellbeing of your marriage and family. We are meant to be one with our spouse—to work together as a team, but again—we are one union or team, made of separate parts. So just like anything that has more than one part, each part has different functions and requires different things to operate at peak levels. For example, putting oil in the engine of a car would ruin it, but that doesn't mean the car doesn't require oil at all.

Don't be afraid to admit you need some 'me time', and don't be afraid to take it. You and your marriage need it and deserve it. BUT…yes, there's almost always a 'but'…

We need to be careful not to use 'me time' as an excuse for pulling away from our spouse, avoiding conflict, or as a method of dealing with hurt, anger, disappointment, and other relationship problems that can quickly destroy a marriage if not dealt with promptly and properly. 'Me time' should leave you feeling refreshed and when it's over, you should be looking forward to coming back together with your spouse and family. You should view your time as time spent for making your marriage and home stronger.

Prayer

LORD, you know me. You know what I need to nourish and nurture about myself to make me a better spouse. Give me the wisdom, energy, and time to do so. Help me to be me more like you, a better friend, lover, and helper to my spouse. In Jesus' name, amen.

Week Forty-three: Me Days

TASK 1
HOW MUCH 'ME TIME' DO YOU TAKE FOR YOURSELF IN A WEEK? MONTH?

Souls in Harmony

TASK 2 — HOW DO YOU SPEND THIS TIME?

_____
_____
_____
_____
_____
_____
_____
_____
_____
_____
_____
_____
_____
_____
_____
_____
_____

Week Forty-three: Me Days

TASK 3
DO EITHER OF YOU EVER RESENT THE OTHER PERSON'S 'ME TIME'? IF SO, WHY?

_____
_____
_____
_____
_____
_____
_____
_____
_____
_____
_____
_____
_____
_____
_____
_____
_____
_____
_____
_____
_____
_____

TASK 4

WHAT CAN YOU DO TO USE 'ME TIME' TO MAKE YOUR MARRIAGE STRONGER THAT YOU AREN'T CURRENTLY DOING?

_____
_____
_____
_____
_____
_____
_____
_____
_____
_____
_____
_____
_____
_____
_____
_____
_____
_____
_____

Week Forty-three: Me Days

TASK 5 — IF YOU DON'T TAKE TIME FOR YOURSELF, WHY DON'T YOU?

_____
_____
_____
_____
_____
_____
_____
_____
_____
_____
_____
_____
_____
_____
_____
_____
_____
_____
_____
_____
_____

TASK 6: IF YOU ARE MISUSING 'ME TIME', WHAT ARE YOU GOING TO DO TO GET YOURSELF AND YOUR MARRIAGE BACK INTO ITS PROPER PLACE IN YOUR LIFE?

Week Forty-four: Thanks for Making Me...

Do not neglect to do good and to share what you have, for such sacrifices are pleasing to God. ~Hebrews 13:6

Jason and Jessica were married—legally. But the piece of paper was about all their marriage consisted of. They went out to eat together, but after he paid the bill (so people wouldn't gossip), she paid him her portion of the bill. They went grocery shopping together…sort of. He had his cart and she had hers. They paid for their own groceries, and those things either of them cooked to eat together were split in half once they got home.

It should come as no surprise that their marriage didn't last much beyond their third anniversary.
Nine years later Jessica is happily remarried and the mother of two. She and her husband share everything—even social media accounts.
Nine years later Jason is still unmarried and has been in and out of more relationships than probably even he can count.
Sharing is essential in a marriage. Not just groceries and restaurant tabs, though. As husbands and wives, we need to share our thoughts, our feelings, our wisdom, and our skills. It is by helping each other; picking up the slack in one another's weaknesses and letting each other take the lead where we are

strongest, that we make our marriage one that is strong and unified.

Moses had the support of Zipporah when he returned to Egypt to rescue the Israelites. Even though she was not of the same nationality, she shared her husband's desire to obey God.

Joseph and Mary shared their resolve to face the gossip and raised eyebrows of their townspeople. They shared the knowledge and awe that they had been chosen by God to raise the Messiah. They shared fear, anticipation, questions, and gratitude that came with being chosen for such a task.

Job and Mrs. Job shared immeasurable grief. And when you really read the book of Job, you come to see that they also shared doubts, frustration, and anger toward God. Job's faith and respect of God's holiness won out over Mrs. Job's anger, though, and because he shared that faith with her, God blessed them with another family.

When we look at these examples of sharing, it should cause us to evaluate how well we are sharing our lives with one another. It's one thing to sit at the table together each evening (which is important), but it's quite another to share your deepest thoughts, feelings, and time with your spouse. So ask yourself...

How much do you share with your spouse?

How willingly do you share with your spouse?

What do you withhold from your spouse?

What do you wish your spouse would share with you, that he/she doesn't?

How would sharing more make your marriage better?

Week Forty-four: Thanks for Making Me...

TASK 1
DO YOU AND YOUR SPOUSE SHARE A BANK ACCOUNT? WHY OR WHY NOT?

_____
_____
_____
_____
_____
_____
_____
_____
_____
_____
_____
_____
_____
_____
_____
_____
_____
_____
_____

Souls in Harmony

TASK 2

MAKE A LIST OF THREE OR FOUR THINGS YOUR SPOUSE DOES BETTER THAN YOU AND THREE OR FOUR THINGS YOU DO BETTER THAN YOUR SPOUSE.

_____
_____
_____
_____
_____
_____
_____
_____
_____
_____
_____
_____
_____
_____
_____
_____
_____
_____

Week Forty-four: Thanks for Making Me…

TASK 3
SHARE YOUR LISTS WITH ONE ANOTHER AND MAKE TIME TO DO EACH OF THESE THINGS TOGETHER.

Use the time and experiences helping one another, praising each other for your individual talents, and assuring each other that you will always be there to work together as a team.

_____
_____
_____
_____
_____
_____
_____
_____
_____
_____
_____
_____
_____
_____
_____
_____
_____
_____
_____
_____
_____

TASK 4 INVITE OTHER COUPLES OVER FOR A GAME NIGHT; PLAYING TEAM GAMES LIKE CHARADES, TABOO, CATCHPHRASE, ETC. INSTEAD OF THE USUAL MEN AGAINST WOMEN, THOUGH, LET EACH COUPLE BE A TEAM.

Week Forty-four: Thanks for Making Me…

TASK 5

CHOOSE A COUPLE OF ACTIVITIES TO DO ON DATES THAT REQUIRE TEAMWORK. EXAMPLES: CANOEING, ESCAPE ROOMS, JIGSAW PUZZLES, CORN MAZE

Week Forty-five: Don't Jump

But test everything; hold fast what is good. ~1st Thessalonians 5:21

Many a relationship has been fractured, if not broken beyond repair, because of assumptions. He assumes she doesn't love him because she doesn't do 'this' or 'that'. She assumes he doesn't find her attractive and desirable anymore because she didn't lose her baby weight. He assumes she doesn't appreciate his hard work like the pretty coworker does, because she's always taking care of the kids. She assumes he doesn't appreciate all she does at home, because he never says 'thank you' or compliments her efforts. He assumes she doesn't understand how hard he works to keep their finances above water, because he doesn't realize the time and energy she puts into couponing, shopping clearance racks, and turning down invitations to go to lunch with her friends because she doesn't want to over extend their budget. She assumes he doesn't care about their home because he puts off mowing the yard until it can't be ignored and the faucet has leaked for months, but he doesn't miss a single soccer practice or game their daughter has.

The Greek word used in this week's verse for 'test' is dokimazete. It means to prove or examine, which is quite the opposite of assuming and jumping to conclusions, wouldn't you agree? And that's exactly what we need to do when we have questions, doubts, and fears in our marriage. Or in any circumstance, for that matter!

Jumping to conclusions is like trying to open a carton of ice cream or a box of cereal from the bottom. You'll eventually get it open, but it will be more difficult and a lot messier than doing it the right way. And just in case there's any question in your mind about what the right way for addressing assumptions, here it is: ask questions (even the hard ones), be transparent with your thoughts and feelings, and tell the other person what you need from them.

It really is that simple. It is also completely worth swallowing some pride and possible hearing some things you don't want to hear. The best marriages are those that are shared between two people who are honest, vulnerable, trusting, and trustworthy. Be that marriage.

Prayer

God, thank you for my spouse. Thank you for the life we've shared so far. I ask now that you keep us accountable to you and to one another, and that you will fill us with grace and wisdom to be honest and open with one another now and forever. Amen.

TASK 1
WHEN HAVE YOU JUMPED TO CONCLUSIONS IN YOUR MARRIAGE? WHY? WHAT HAPPENED?

___

Week Forty-five: Don't Jump

TASK 2
IS THERE ANYTHING YOU FEEL YOUR SPOUSE HAS A FALSE ASSUMPTION ABOUT REGARDING YOU PERSONALLY AND YOUR MARRIAGE RELATIONSHIPS?

_____
_____
_____
_____
_____
_____
_____
_____
_____
_____
_____
_____
_____
_____
_____
_____
_____
_____
_____
_____

TASK 3 SET ASIDE AN AFTERNOON OR EVENING ALONE TO ADDRESS THESE ISSUES. BE HONEST, GRACIOUS, AND DO SO WITH THE DESIRE AND INTENT TO BECOME CLOSER THAN EVER.

_____
_____
_____
_____
_____
_____
_____
_____
_____
_____
_____
_____
_____
_____
_____
_____
_____

TASK 4
SPEND TIME THIS WEEK PRAYING TOGETHER FOR A MORE TRANSPARENT AND COMMUNICATIVE MARRIAGE.

_____
_____
_____
_____
_____
_____
_____
_____
_____
_____
_____
_____
_____
_____
_____
_____
_____
_____
_____
_____
_____
_____
_____

Souls in Harmony

TASK 5 DON'T ASSUME YOU ARE THE ONLY COUPLE THAT NEEDS HELP. TAKE OPPORTUNITIES TO SHARE WHAT THIS DEVOTIONAL BOOK IS DOING FOR YOUR PERSONAL RELATIONSHIP WITH GOD AND FOR YOUR MARRIAGE. RECOMMEND THE BOOK TO FRIENDS. GO ONLINE AND WRITE A REVIEW THAT INCLUDES A TESTIMONY OF HOW IT HAS HELPED YOU AND YOUR SPOUSE.

_____
_____
_____
_____
_____
_____
_____
_____
_____
_____
_____
_____
_____
_____
_____
_____
_____
_____
_____
_____

Week Forty-five: Don't Jump

Week Forty-six: Better Together

Two are better than one, because they have a good return for their labor: If either of them falls down, one can help the other up. ~Ecclesiastes 4:9-10

A couple of weeks ago you focused on the importance of sharing and how detrimental it is to the health of your marriage. This week we want to continue that thought. This week the focus is going to be on working together. Not just physically, but emotionally and spiritually. Some couples enjoy working together. They know how to work with and around each other's likes and dislikes, strengths and weaknesses, and levels of patience to accomplish all sorts of things. For example, one couple I know still in the throes of raising small children, each have their 'things' they do best when it comes to the kids and housework. Nick is great with bath time, lawn work, and taking the boys and their friends to play. Charlene doesn't like driving in the city, so she hates the distraction of the kids' noise in the car, an injury from a car accident when she was twelve, makes it painful for her to kneel over the bathtub, and she enjoys yard work, but is intimidated by the riding mower, so she sticks to the flowerbeds and their little vegetable garden.

BUT…you wouldn't catch either of them shopping for boys'

clothes and gifts without the other, attending a family event alone, or paying the monthly bills. These two also have tons of fun cooking together, serving on a couple of ministry teams at their church, and bedtime reading with the boys, and just hanging out after the boys are in bed are their favorite times of the day. That's working together. Not always doing everything together, but knowing they are getting it all done by working as a team. It's not always that easy, though. Couples whose marriage includes military deployment, extended travel away from home, or one in which physical disabilities prevent one spouse from taking part in many (most) activities, present the need for a whole different way of doing things. When a spouse is hundreds or thousands of miles away, you can't pay bills together, go shopping together, or depend on your mate to help out around the house or take the kids for a few hours. Or when your spouse is a quadriplegic, he/she can't mow the lawn or make a quick run to the store for milk and diapers.

Does that mean these marriages can't be the team they are supposed to be? No, it does not. Just like no two people are alike, no two marriages are alike. The only unchanged variable is God. And as long as God is your personal number-one priority, and as long as he is at the head and is the core of your marriage, don't worry. God will give you the understanding and direction you need to be a team. Your own unique team that works on love, trust, and commitment.

Prayer

God, thank you for the man/woman you gave me to be my mate. Help us to not take each other for granted or to ignore one another's efforts to help. Make us true partners in life. In Jesus' name, amen.

Week Forty-six: Better Together

TASK 1

What are your strong points—physically, emotionally, and spiritually? How can you better use these things to enhance your marriage?

_____
_____
_____
_____
_____
_____
_____
_____
_____
_____
_____
_____
_____
_____
_____
_____
_____
_____
_____
_____
_____

TASK 2
WHAT DO YOU CONSIDER TO BE YOUR SPOUSE'S STRONG POINTS?

_____
_____
_____
_____
_____
_____
_____
_____
_____
_____
_____
_____
_____
_____
_____
_____
_____
_____
_____

Week Forty-six: Better Together

TASK 3
SPEND SOME TIME THIS WEEK WRITING YOUR SPOUSE A THANK-YOU NOTE FOR THEIR HELP AND SUPPORT.

_____
_____
_____
_____
_____
_____
_____
_____
_____
_____
_____
_____
_____
_____
_____
_____
_____
_____
_____
_____

Souls in Harmony

TASK 4 ASK YOUR SPOUSE TO HELP YOU WITH SOMETHING THIS WEEK. REMEMBER: FEELING NEEDED AND APPRECIATED IS A HUGE "I LOVE YOU".

Week Forty-six: Better Together

Week Forty-seven: Relaaaaax

And he said to them, "Come away by yourselves to a desolate place and rest a while." For many were coming and going, and they had no leisure even to eat. ~Mark 6:31

Jesus is talking to his disciples in this week's verse. He is warning them against getting so busy doing ministry that they forget to take care of themselves. They weren't even taking time to eat!

Sound familiar? How many times have you worked through lunch so you could take off early to do something with the kids? But then you were so hungry, your blood sugar levels turned you into a big old grouch.

Or what about all those times you stressed yourself out trying to second-guess what your wife wants for Valentine's Day (instead of taking the logical route and asking her)? And then there's all the overtime you put into Thanksgiving dinner for your husband's family and all he has to say on the matter is, "Don't worry about it," or "I don't see why you're making such a big deal out of it.".

We also spend massive amounts of time and energy working to meet expenses vs. paring our expenses down to meeting our income AND giving us more time to relax and enjoy each other and the non-things in life that really matter.

Souls in Harmony

The Bible has much to say on the matter of rest, relaxation, reducing stress, and taking time to just 'be'. In fact, the third commandment is to devote an entire day each week for rest, renewal, and focusing on God and your relationship with him. It's called Sabbath.

Take the next few minutes reading and meditating on these verses. While none of them are specifically meant to address the need for restfulness in a marriage relationship, the relevancy is still there, because the Bible is always relevant in all things.

The Lord is my shepherd, I lack nothing. He makes me lie down in green pastures, he leads me beside quiet waters, he refreshes my soul. ~Psalm 23:1-3

Come to me, all who labor and are heavy laden, and I will give you rest. ~Matthew 11:28

It is in vain that you rise up early and go late to rest, eating the bread of anxious toil; for he gives to his beloved sleep. ~Psalm 127:2

So then, there remains a Sabbath rest for the people of God, for whoever has entered God's rest has also rested from his works as God did from his. ~Hebrews 4:9-10

"Six days you shall work, but on the seventh day you shall rest. In plowing time and in harvest you shall rest. ~Exodus 34:21

Why do you think God wants, aka, requires us to rest?

It's simple, really. Because we need it. He knows the human body. After all, he created it. It is his masterpiece. One of millions upon millions, actually. He knows that when we aren't relaxed and well-rested that we make mistakes. Our thinking isn't as rational as it should be. We react rather than respond. We say things we don't mean. We take unnecessary risks. We turn to things that don't satisfy in an effort to be satisfied. We fail to take responsibility for our own actions. We withdraw. We become defensive and confrontational out of an attitude of self-preservation.

Sound familiar? This isn't the person you want to be. The life you want to live. The marriage you want to have. So, don't let it be.

Prayer

God, slow me down. Give me the mindset to rest in you and with my spouse. Give me the mindset to put the world aside to focus on honoring you in all ways—especially in how we do marriage.
Amen.

TASK 1
ON A SCALE OF ONE TO TEN, HOW STRESSED WOULD YOU SAY YOU ARE? *TEN BEING YOUR STRESS LEVEL IS OVER THE TOP.

_____
_____
_____
_____
_____
_____
_____
_____
_____
_____
_____
_____
_____
_____
_____
_____
_____
_____
_____

Week Forty-seven: Relaaaaax

TASK 2 WHY? WHAT ARE THE REASONS FOR THE STRESS IN YOUR LIFE?

TASK 3
WHAT ARE SOME PRACTICAL AND REALISTIC THINGS YOU CAN DO TO REDUCE THE AMOUNT OF STRESS IN YOUR LIFE?

___

___

___

___

___

___

___

___

___

___

___

___

___

___

___

___

___

___

___

___

Week Forty-seven: Relaaaaax

TASK 4
SPEND TIME TALKING TO ONE ANOTHER ABOUT THE STRESS IN YOUR LIFE AND THE REASONS FOR IT. TALK ABOUT THE ANSWERS TO QUESTION 3 AND PUT TOGETHER A PLAN TO ACTUALLY DO THE THINGS ON THE LIST.

_____
_____
_____
_____
_____
_____
_____
_____
_____
_____
_____
_____
_____
_____
_____
_____
_____
_____
_____
_____
_____
_____

TASK 5

MONEY IS ALMOST ALWAYS THE NUMBER-ONE STRESS FACTOR IN A MARRIAGE. WOULD YOU DESCRIBE YOUR SITUATION AS WORKING TO MEET YOUR BUDGET, OR BUDGETING TO MEET YOUR INCOME?

Week Forty-seven: Relaaaaax

TASK 6: WHAT ARE YOUR FAVORITE WAYS TO RELAX? HOW OFTEN DO YOU DO THESE THINGS?

No where in the Bible does it say the Sabbath is no longer necessary or desired by God. Working together, choose a day for your Sabbath. It doesn't always or even ever have to be Sunday. Some people have no choice but to work on Sunday. It also doesn't have to be the same day each week. Use the day to do things that relax you and make you feel rested, revived, more aware of God's presence in your life.

Week Forty-eight: The Buck Stops Here

Therefore, if anyone is in Christ, he is a new creation. The old has passed away; behold, the new has come. ~2nd Corinthians 5:17

A study conducted a few years ago at the University of Utah concluded that adults whose parents divorced when they were children, are much more likely to get divorced, too. The study broke it down ever further by revealing that if one spouse in a marriage comes from a broken home, the marriage is twice as likely to fail as a marriage in which neither spouse comes from a broken home. If both spouses come from a broken home, the marriage is three times as likely to end in divorce as a marriage between two people whose parents are not divorced.

This study is not the only one of its kind. Over the course of the past few decades, several such studies have been done. Each time the results are basically the same. But why? Why would someone who has been through the pain of their parents' divorce want to put themselves or anyone else through the same pain? The answer can usually be attributed to simply this: they don't know anything else. They live what they learn. Remember—history repeats itself. Right?
It does, unless we learn from it. Like Lucas did.
Lucas has every reason you can think of for being a rotten husband, father, and man. Raised in an atmosphere of abuse

and neglect, he witnessed his parents try to sell him. He saw them steal money from his wallet to buy pills and alcohol. He stared his father down was the man held a gun to his head. He secretly lived on the streets until one night he finally confessed the situation to his girlfriend, whose dad immediately drove to get him and bring him home with them.

Nine years later, Lucas is a loving and devoted husband to that same girl, an equally loving and devoted father to their five and two year-old daughters, is a decorated military officer, and a faithful man of God whose example is admired and respected by everyone who knows him.

History will never repeat itself here, because Lucas learned that the old ways don't have to follow you. God takes the old and gives you new…when you let him.

Not every situation is as dire as this one. Other situations that call for the generational 'old' being put to rest include:

- Always doing holidays the same…no exceptions. There are times when you need to say no to your parents and do holidays in a way that is best for your marriage and your family.
- The family business. As difficult as this can be, if a family business is wreaking havoc on your marriage, it's time to choose marriage over generational expectations.
- Your address. If your marriage and family will be stronger and healthier living away from extended family, move. Everyone will be better for it.

This isn't to say that all generational bridges are bad—that there is no history worth repeating. Just take the time to measure it against the Word of God. Can you say yes, when measured against Philippians 4:8, which says, "Finally, brothers and sisters, whatever is true, whatever is noble, whatever is right, whatever is pure, whatever is lovely, whatever is admirable—if anything is excellent or praiseworthy—think about such things."

Prayer

God, give us the courage and strength to pattern our lives and our marriage after you and your Word. Nothing more. Nothing less. In the name of Jesus, amen.

TASK 1
HOW WOULD YOU SAY YOUR MARRIAGE COMPARES TO THAT OF YOUR PARENTS? YOUR IN-LAWS?

_____
_____
_____
_____
_____
_____
_____
_____
_____
_____
_____
_____
_____
_____
_____
_____
_____
_____
_____
_____

Souls in Harmony

TASK 2

HOW DO THE SIMILARITIES MAKE YOU FEEL? ARE YOU GRATEFUL? SAD? RESIGNED? DETERMINED TO CHANGE THE COURSE OF YOUR FUTURE?

_____
_____
_____
_____
_____
_____
_____
_____
_____
_____
_____
_____
_____
_____
_____
_____
_____
_____
_____

Week Forty-eight: The Buck Stops Here

TASK 3 ARE YOU FEELING TRAPPED BY ANY TYPE OF GENERATIONAL TRADITION YOU AND YOUR SPOUSE ARE EXPECTED TO ADHERE TO? EXPLAIN.

_____
_____
_____
_____
_____
_____
_____
_____
_____
_____
_____
_____
_____
_____
_____
_____
_____
_____
_____
_____

Souls in Harmony

TASK 4 WHAT, IF ANYTHING, WILL YOU DO TO CHANGE?

_____
_____
_____
_____
_____
_____
_____
_____
_____
_____
_____
_____
_____
_____
_____
_____
_____
_____
_____

Week Forty-eight: The Buck Stops Here

TASK 5: WHAT GENERATIONAL TRADITIONS DO YOU RESPECT AND EMBRACE IN YOUR MARRIAGE? WHY?

Souls in Harmony

Week Forty-nine: Spring Cleaning

For where your treasure is, there your heart will be also. ~Matthew 6:21

If you aren't familiar with Jesus' encounter with the man the Bible calls The Rich Young Ruler, here it is in a nutshell: the rich young man asks Jesus what he must do to receive eternal life with God. Jesus told the young man he must keep all the commandments. When the young man replied that he did—that he had since he was just a boy—Jesus then added, "Sell everything you have and give it to the poor, then come and follow me." The young man turned and left with a heavy heart because he couldn't bring himself to do that. He couldn't bring himself to give up his wealth and material possessions for Jesus. For eternal life in heaven. We understand that this passage is speaking to us on a spiritual level, but it is also applicable to marriage. When we value something other than our marriage, it suffers. It might possible even die—if not visibly, then emotionally. As husbands and wives, we need to safeguard them by rolling up our sleeves and doing a little spring, summer, fall, and winter cleaning to make sure nothing—tangible or intangible—is taking up too much space in our marriage. Some of the things we need to watch out for include:

- Work. It's necessary, but it's not your life.
- The kids. Again, being a parent is the most awesome and humbling job you'll ever have. One that you should take seriously and pour yourself into. But in the process, don't neglect one another. One day those kids are going to be grown and gone, and you are going to need each other. You don't want to find yourself living with a stranger.
- Money. It's not everything, so don't let it cost you that (everything).
- Outside relationships. They are necessary, healthy, and fun. But they should never become more important to you than your marriage relationship. They should be a little accessory to life—nothing more.
- Hobbies. Hiding in, under, or behind a hobby to escape a problematic or lackluster marriage only makes marriage more lackluster and problematic.
- Apathy. Believing things are the way they are because that's the way they are…. Not true! God is ready, willing, and able to bring life and joy, and excitement back into your marriage. Let him.
- Material possessions. Houses don't make homes. Stuff doesn't guarantee happiness. Presents are nothing if not partnered with your presence. When is the last time you cleaned your house?

Prayer

LORD, help me see myself honestly and without bias. Help me recognize the things I am putting in front of you and in front of my marriage. Give me the strength to not stop there, though, but to get rid of these things, or to put them in their proper place in my life—after you and after my marriage. In the name of Jesus, amen.

Souls in Harmony

TASK 1
LOOKING AT THE LIST OF JUNK YOU NEED TO CLEAN OUT OF YOUR MARRIAGE, WHICH OF THESE THINGS DO YOU TEND TO HANG ON TO?

_____
_____
_____
_____
_____
_____
_____
_____
_____
_____
_____
_____
_____
_____
_____
_____
_____
_____

Week Forty-nine: Spring Cleaning

TASK 2
HOW HAVE THESE THINGS AFFECTED YOUR RELATIONSHIP?

_____
_____
_____
_____
_____
_____
_____
_____
_____
_____
_____
_____
_____
_____
_____
_____
_____
_____
_____
_____

TASK 3
IF YOU COULD CHANGE THREE THINGS ABOUT YOUR MARRIAGE, WHAT WOULD THEY BE?

_____
_____
_____
_____
_____
_____
_____
_____
_____
_____
_____
_____
_____
_____
_____
_____
_____

Week Forty-nine: Spring Cleaning

TASK 4 WHAT'S STOPPING YOU? GET DOWN ON YOUR KNEES AND ASK GOD TO OPEN THE DOORS TO CHANGE. TALK TO YOUR SPOUSE AND TELL HIM/HER WHAT YOU NEED AND WANT. START CLEANING HOUSE TO MAKE YOUR DESIRES A REALITY.

Week Fifty: It's not All About Either of You

Before destruction a man's heart is haughty, but humility comes before honor. ~Proverbs 18:12

There are a lot of quirky, humorous, and wise sayings we like to quote and claim as our mantras or 'mission statements', one of which is "Happy wife…happy life".

Talk about selfish! What about happy husband, happy home? Just because it doesn't rhyme doesn't mean it doesn't matter. It matters a lot. Marriage isn't about meeting the needs of just one person at the expense of another. God's command for husbands to love their wives as Christ loves the church isn't about catering to their every whim and fancy. Wives are to submit to their husband's Godly authority. And let's not forget that we are to do to others as we would have them do to us (Luke 6:31).

It is incredibly easy to become selfish and self-centered in today's society. We are bombarded with advice to take what's ours, to not let anyone walk on us or get ahead of us, to look out for number one, and all sorts of others like them. It is even fair to say the Christians are even more susceptible to such thoughts. Satan works overtime to tempt us to fall for these lies, and sadly, we often do.

Guarding your hearts, and ultimately your marriage, against selfishness and entitlement is one of those essentials you cannot ignore. It is also something you have to work at diligently and consistently.

One of the most vivid examples of this in the Bible is seen in King Herod. We know he was about as Godless as they come, but he went against his better judgement just to please his woman. He murdered John the Baptist in cold blood just because she asked him to (Matthew 14).

Another example is seen in Abraham and Sarah. Had Abraham not given into Sarah's insistence to have a child with her servant, Hagar, the world we live in would be a very different place.

Convincing your husband to take a surrogate wife and killing people you are mad aren't the issues we deal with these days, but that doesn't make what we do deal with any less dangerous to a marriage. The things that tend to be most threatening to the humility factor in a marriage these days include:

- Pressures of social media on us (especially women) to keep up with their peers by projecting an image of wealth and materialism
- Pressures from mainstream media that sexuality and attractiveness are equal to outward appearance.
- An insistence for equality in all matters using a distorted perception of what equality really is.
- Chauvinism.
- Distrust and revenge
- Entitlement that comes from being spoiled by your parents
- Pressure from the professional arena to project a certain image
- Misconceptions about marriage in general
- Poor role models for marriage and bringing these experiences into your own marriage

If you want a slogan or mantra for your marriage, why not choose something that will inspire both of you to be your best self—something like "Marriage is a verb—not a noun. It's something you do—not something you get."

TASK 1 DO SOMETHING NICE AND UNEXPECTED FOR YOUR SPOUSE EVERY DAY THIS WEEK.

Week Fifty: It's not All About Either of You

TASK 2

HOW MANY TIMES A DAY DO YOU SAY 'ME' OR 'I' WHEN TALKING TO YOUR SPOUSE, VS. 'WE' AND 'US'?

___

Souls in Harmony

TASK 3

WHAT IS THE REASON FOR MOST OF THE DISAGREEMENTS AND ARGUMENTS YOU HAVE WITH YOUR SPOUSE? IS IT BECAUSE YOU AREN'T GETTING YOUR WAY?

___

___

___

___

___

___

___

___

___

___

___

___

___

___

___

___

___

___

___

___

Week Fifty: It's not All About Either of You

TASK 4
WHO IS MOST LIKELY TO COMPROMISE OR GIVE IN WHEN THE TWO OF YOU DON'T AGREE?

_____
_____
_____
_____
_____
_____
_____
_____
_____
_____
_____
_____
_____
_____
_____
_____
_____
_____
_____

TASK 5
HOW WELL DO YOU FEEL THE TWO OF YOU COMPROMISE? DISCUSS THIS WITH YOUR SPOUSE.

_____
_____
_____
_____
_____
_____
_____
_____
_____
_____
_____
_____
_____
_____
_____
_____
_____
_____
_____

Week Fifty: It's not All About Either of You

Week Fifty-one: Close to You

He who finds a wife finds a good thing and obtains favor from the Lord. ~Proverbs 18:22

Country music star, Clint Black, wrote and recorded a beautiful song back in 1997 titled, "Something That We Do". Part of the lyrics go like this…

…Love is certain, love is kind
Love is yours and love is mine
But it isn't something that we find
It's something that we do

It's holding tight, lettin' go
It's flying high and laying low
Let your strongest feelings show
And your weakness, too
It's a little and a lot to ask
An endless and a welcome task
Love isn't something that we have
It's something that we do…
We help to make each other all that we can be
We can find our strength and inspiration independently
The way we work together is what sets our love apart
So closely that we can't tell where I end and where you start
The words to this song could have easily been written for a few couples we read about in the Bible. Zechariah and Elizabeth

stood by one another through the pain of infertility, Zechariah's responsibility as a priest, his temporary disability when he questioned the validity of God's messenger, and the social pressure of going against tradition when they named their son. Adam and Eve had no one to pattern their marriage after and we all know they made mistakes. But they were God-made for each other and took their union seriously. They went through being chastised by God, being displaced from their home, and the grief of knowing one son killed another…and they went through it together.

What about you and your spouse? Is your intimacy level one that blurs the lines between where you end and your spouse begins? Are you fully committed to work together to have your best life? Is love something you do?

Creating a strong foundation of intimacy isn't something that just happens. The very word intimacy is defined by using words like attachment, confidentiality, and togetherness. Those things require your physical, emotional, and mental participation. Think of it like this: wanting a cup of hot tea or coffee when you come in out of the cold isn't enough to actually get you what you want. You have to do something…a lot of somethings.

- Talk. Casual conversation, meaningful conversation. Musings (vocalized thoughts).
- Confide your deepest thoughts, concerns, questions, fears, and dreams knowing you will be listened to, respected, and heard.
- Touch—casual, comforting, playful, affectionate, sexual.
- Laugh. Cry.
- Share your accomplishments, secrets, money, material stuff.
- Worship together. Pray together. Serve together. Mature in Christ together.

A wife of noble character who can find? She is worth far more

Week Fifty-one: Close to You

than rubies. Her husband has full confidence in her and lacks nothing of value. She brings him good, not harm, all the days of her life.

Full confidence in one another. Bringing good not harm to one another. Intimacy is the telling factor that decides whether two people are merely married, or in a marriage. Which would you prefer?

Prayer

LORD, help my spouse and I draw closer to one another and closer to you, so that our marriage can be a fulfilling experience and a shining example to others. Help us feel safe enough with each other to share every detail of our lives. In your son's name, amen.

TASK 1
DO YOU OR YOUR SPOUSE STRUGGLE WITH INTIMACY OUTSIDE OF SEX? IF SO, WHY?

_____
_____
_____
_____
_____
_____
_____
_____
_____
_____
_____
_____
_____
_____
_____
_____
_____
_____
_____
_____
_____

Week Fifty-one: Close to You

TASK 2
HOW DO YOU THINK YOUR MARRIAGE WOULD BENEFIT FROM BEING MORE INTIMATE?

_____
_____
_____
_____
_____
_____
_____
_____
_____
_____
_____
_____
_____
_____
_____
_____
_____
_____
_____
_____
_____

Souls in Harmony

TASK 3

When you confide in your spouse, does he/she make you feel insignificant? Does he/she make you feel your thoughts and feelings are unreasonable or unimportant? Or do they listen attentively, making you feel safe and hopeful?

_____
_____
_____
_____
_____
_____
_____
_____
_____
_____
_____
_____
_____
_____
_____
_____
_____
_____

Week Fifty-one: Close to You

TASK 4

Choose one of the forms of intimacy listed above (talking, confiding, touching, emotional connection, sharing, spiritual growth) each week for the next six weeks. Spend a few minutes each day developing intimacy with one another in this way.

___
___
___
___
___
___
___
___
___
___
___
___
___
___
___
___
___
___
___
___
___
___

Week Fifty-two: In Pursuit of Love

As a lily among brambles, so is my love among the young women.
~Song of Solomon 2:2

Rebekah 'fell for' Isaac when she saw him praying and meditating in the middle of a field. There was just something about a man spending time alone with God that told her he was 'a keeper'. The feelings were mutual for Isaac, when he saw Rebekah climbing down off her camel. Genesis 24 simply says, he saw her and loved her.

There doesn't seem to be anything too romantic about their relationship, does there? It was basically an arranged marriage in which Isaac just happened to fall in love with his bride. The same can be said for most couples in the Bible. Other than the bride and groom in the Song of Solomon, romance doesn't seem to be of any significance.
So, is it? Is romance actually important in a marriage?
Romance, as in flowers, candlelight dinners, candy, and sweep-me-off-my-feet kind of date, is not included in God's precepts for marriage. But before you guys start high-fiving too much and sighing in relief thinking you've just been taken off the hook, keep reading…
The exclusive nature of love between a husband and wife needs to be nurtured and fed. It's favorite food—romance.

Being romantic with your spouse is about so much more than sex, Romance is like the marriage meal, with sex being dessert. Romance is…

- The little signals you send one another while in public that no one else sees or understands (a wink, nod, or grin, the squeeze of a hand, a light touch, or even a 'secret' word or phrase.
- Unexpectedly doing something for your spouse to make their day easier, brighter, safer (examples: folding the laundry, reading to them while they fall asleep, drawing them a hot bath, watching their favorite movie (even if it's your least favorite).
- Holding hands just because.
- Chivalry and good manners.
- Commenting on their beauty and complimenting their actions.
- Remembering important dates and events.
- Romance is also bit like an insurance policy. When you romance your spouse, they won't question where your thoughts and loyalties lie. Like Isaac and Rebekah you'll just know.

Prayer

LORD, help me understand that romance is an important tool of validation in my marriage. Help me 'do' romance well so that my husband/wife will feel special and reassured that our love is the forever exclusive love meant for marriage. Amen

PART 1 MAKE A LIST OF ALL YOUR SPOUSE'S FAVORITES: FOOD, SNACK, MOVIE, BOOK, STORE, OUTSIDE ACTIVITY, MOVIE, SPORTS TEAM, COFFEE, ICE CREAM, SPORT, HOBBIES, ETC.

_____
_____
_____
_____
_____
_____
_____
_____
_____
_____
_____
_____
_____
_____
_____
_____

Week Fifty-two: In Pursuit of Love

PART 2 CHOOSE ONE THING OFF THE LIST EVERY DAY FOR THE NEXT FEW DAYS AND ROMANCE HIM/HER BY TREATING THEM TO THESE THINGS.

___

Souls in Harmony

PART 3 TELL EACH OTHER THREE ROMANTIC GESTURES YOU WOULD ENJOY BEING TREATED TO. DO THESE THINGS FOR EACH OTHER—BUT TRY TO SURPRISE THEM.

Week Fifty-two: In Pursuit of Love

Closing Comments: Fifty-two weeks

One year of using God's Word and examples of people just like you to grow closer to God and to one another. To take your marriage to the next level of God's expectations and design for marriage. It is my hope and prayer that you will continue to use what you've learned so that you and your marriage will keep going in a positive God-honoring direction. It is also my hope and prayer that you will feel compelled to share this experience with other couples. You can do this by word of mouth and by reviewing the book on sites like Amazon, Barnes and Noble, Good Reads, and other book review sites. I know it sometimes seems futile or unnecessary to do this sort of thing, but it's not. People actually prefer to take the advice of their peers (that's you) when deciding what books to read, coffee makers to buy, or which stores to shop at. So please, be one of those peers.

Finally, don't forget to give this book a review! And don't forget about your free gift. It is my way of saying thank-you for allowing me into your life over the last year. In doing so, you have been in partnership with God to use me to minister to others.

God bless you and your marriage until death do you part!

NOTES

Closing Comments: Fifty-two weeks

NOTES

Printed by Libri Plureos GmbH in Hamburg, Germany